letters
FROM THE FRONT

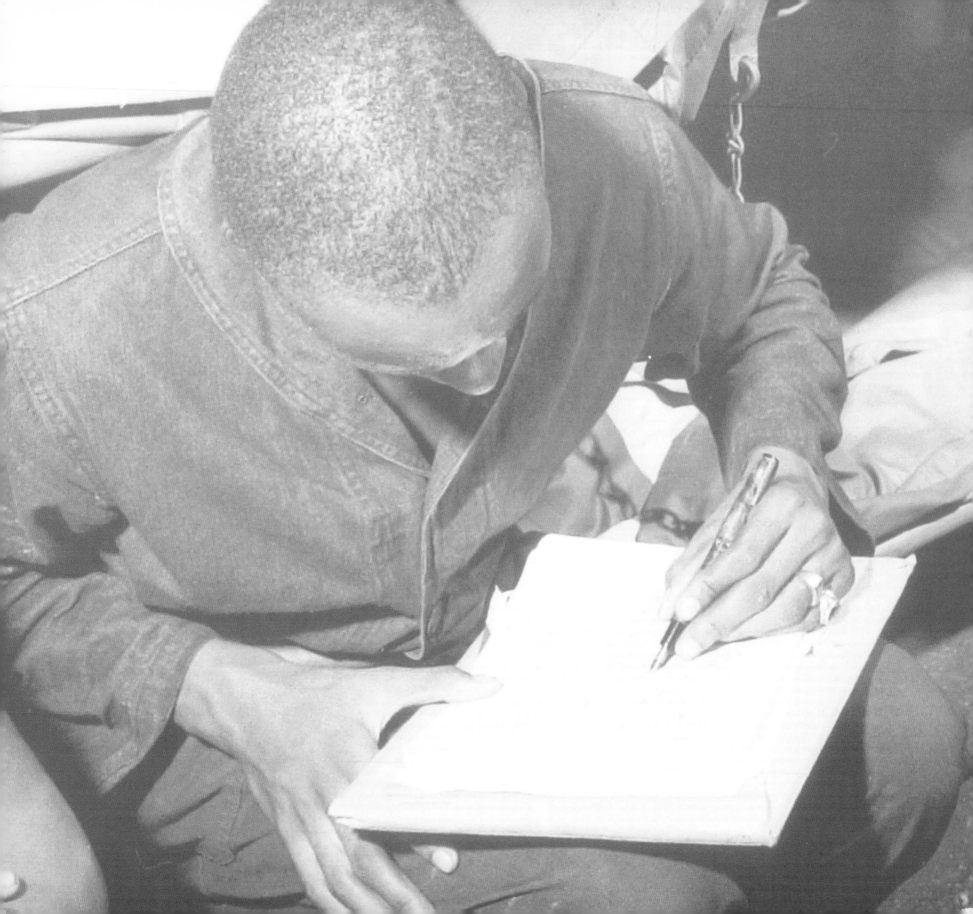

*l*etters
FROM THE FRONT

Judith Millidge

BARRON'S

The publisher would like to state that the
language used within these letters does not reflect
the opinions or beliefs of the publisher, but has
been included to maintain the letters' historical
authenticity.

First edition for the United States and Canada published in
2002 by Barron's Educational Series, Inc.

Produced by PRC Publishing Ltd.,
64 Brewery Road, London N7 9NT

A member of **Chrysalis** Books plc

All inquiries should be addressed to:
Barron's Educational Series, Inc.
250 Wireless Boulevard
Hauppauge, NY 11788
http://www.barronseduc.com

International Standard Book No. 0-7641-5537-7

Library of Congress Catalog Card No. 2001098513.

Printed in Taiwan

9 8 7 6 5 4 3 2 1

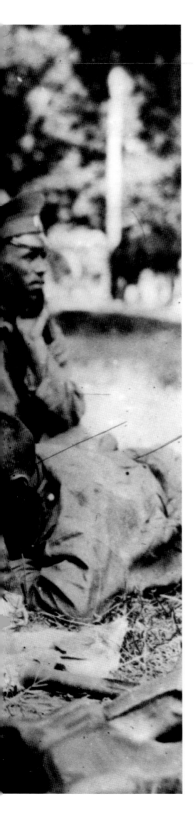

Contents

"The sides facing Cabul are very steep, and covered with huge boulders polished by wind and rain, and of a kind to check any storming party. Perfect cover is afforded to men holding it, and on the summit is a well-built sungar of great thickness, covering a natural cavity in the rocks which has been made bomb-proof by some Afghan engineer, who understood the strength of the point. Fifty men could lie in perfect security behind the sungar or in the hole below it, and could choose their own time for firing at an advancing enemy. Outside the sungar, and a little lower down, is a cave, wherein another strong body of men could hide themselves and act in a similar way, while their flank to the left would be guarded by a broken line of rocks..."

If nothing else, this quotation from a letter written by a British officer in Afghanistan shows the immense value of learning from history. Howard Hensman fought in the Afghan War of 1879 and his descriptions of the rugged land and the fighting habits of the Afghans are remarkably similar to the scenes on television screens in the winter of 2001–2002.

Hensman's letter, and those of countless others, merely underline the fact that the study of military history, the analysis of battle positions and troop movements, and the dry facts of which side won or lost a battle, often mask the true experience of war. Soldiers rarely have a voice until after the shooting has stopped, when their letters and diaries reveal more about the true conditions of battle than statistics or generals' dispatches. Letters home to friends and loved ones are particularly poignant, often revealing prosaic details about the sheer discomfort of life in the front line, while trying to hide the very real danger and almost universal feelings of fear. As historical documents they are fascinating; each one provides a unique insight into an important event, a snapshot of the past, and a glimpse of how people cope with the strains of combat.

What is striking is that although over time weapons and means of killing have become ever more sophisticated, soldiers' emotions do not change. It

Introduction

is clear from their letters that Wellington's soldiers felt exactly the same mixture of pride, apprehension, and determination as their descendants fighting in the deserts of North Africa or the jungles of Vietnam. Soldiers spend a great deal of time waiting for something to happen and boredom is a common problem. "There is also a disgusting delay in getting anything done, when everything should be vigor and activity," complained Major Warre in 1809, as he waited to begin campaigning in the Peninsula. The feelings of the rank and file toward their superiors are often derisory, whether they were cavalry being led "into the Valley of Death" by Lord Cardigan in the Crimea in 1854, or SAS (Special Air Service) troops sent ill-equipped into the deserts of Iraq in 1990. At the same time, the sheer relief at the prospect of being led by a well-respected officer is a universal emotion; soldiers from every war share pride in being part of an army commanded by a man of stature, be he Wellington or Lee, Eisenhower, or Montgomery.

The letters in this book are drawn from a wide variety of sources but are written by men (and a few women) who share a common experience: they have been swept away from their homes and families to fight on behalf of their country. Many were not professional soldiers, but volunteers or conscripts, people whose trades were often far removed from the mechanics of handling a gun and whose temperaments did not naturally incline toward violence. Written by people as diverse as barely literate country folk or sophisticated academics, by lowly privates as well as great leaders, they share one common thread: anxiety. Soldiers sometimes express their fears for their own survival, but more often they worry that their loved ones are worrying about them. Another common theme is their desire to be remembered to friends and relatives; soldiers often do not have the luxury of time and leisure to enable them to write to everyone who sends them a letter, but they want their friends to know they have not forgotten them. Their letters are also peppered with requests for small items to make their lives more comfortable: clothing, tasty food to improve the spartan rations of most armies, photographs or keepsakes of loved ones. Most of all, they look forward to

the time when they will be back with their families, on leave, or even better, the end of the war. Many solders apologize for not writing as often as they'd like, saying that they've been busy, which is both a euphemism and an understatement that disguises their true activities from their families. "Well, I know it's been a long time since my last letter, but as you probably guessed, I've been pretty busy. That doesn't quite describe the intensity, though, really," wrote one Vietnam Marine wryly.

Letters themselves played an almost talismanic role in the lives of correspondents and were often carried in pockets to be read again and again, as physical, tangible reminders of loved ones and home. One American soldier summed up the situation in 1918, writing home that "Mail is almost as essential as a square meal." Draftees wrote to describe their strange new life to their family and friends, trying to make sense of the malign fate that had taken them away from all that they held dear. Volunteers, by contrast, often revel in their new experiences. Letter writing is a cathartic act for many soldiers, allowing them the opportunity to vent their feelings, make sense of their situation, and express sentiments of love and tenderness so very rarely seen on a battlefield.

The Logistics of Communication

By the mid-19th century great value was placed on an efficient field postal service. It was recognized that communications to and from home were good for morale. "War," as William T. Sherman memorably said, "is hell," so the knowledge that friends and relations are thinking of soldiers in action makes the troopers' lives a little less miserable. In 1795, a British act of parliament allowed serving sailors and seamen to send letters from anywhere in the world for the flat rate of one penny, which was the beginning of the British tradition of allowing preferential postal rates for the armed forces. The first British army postmaster, Henry Darlot, was appointed in 1799. It was agreed that "a good and intelligent clerk should accompany the Army to manage the whole correspondence, to facilitate delivery and to collect

Above: A Pony Express rider leaves St. Joseph, Missouri. The Pony Express service that ran from April 1860 to November 1861 kept communication open to California at the beginning of the Civil War.

letters and protect the revenue." Henry Darlot succeeded in making a tidy profit during the two years of his appointment. Ten years later, Wellington appointed a "Post-master within the Army" who was based at army headquarters in Lisbon. Letters passed through the British Packet agent in Lisbon, who put mailbags onto the weekly packet boat bound for Falmouth.

Letter writing became far more widespread during the 19th century as growing numbers of the population became literate and communications improved. Railroads began to snake across continents, the wireless telegraph was first used in battle during the Crimean War, and postal services became increasingly efficient. The wars of the 19th century, the battles of empire, and the American Civil War were all minutely chronicled by their participants and the postal service had to expand to cope with the volume of mail. The sheer logistics of getting a letter to a man in a mobile army unit was taxing, but certainly not impossible. In 1855 during the Crimean War, 1.2 million letters were sent from the battle front to England. The service proved to be erratic at first, but once the army began employing civilian postal officials instead of soldiers, the system became more efficient. In

America, military post remained under civilian control, but each regiment had its own postmaster.

In 1877, the British Secretary for War recommended the formation of a postal corps within the army, consisting of officers and men employed by the Post Office, but who also had military experience. The 24th Middlesex Rifle Volunteers formed the nucleus of the new Army Post Office Corps, which first saw service in 1882 during Gordon's expedition to Egypt. For the first time, families of serving soldiers could expect to hear from their sons, fathers, and brothers when they were away, even if their news was a month or so out of date. And the soldiers themselves could record the sights and sounds of battle and let their families know something of their experiences. The Army Postal Corps expanded to meet the demands of the Boer War (1899–1902). The guerrilla campaign ranged across thousands of square miles and large numbers of troops were required to maintain an efficient postal service. Furthermore, field post offices were not exempt from Boer attack, as they housed stores and often large amounts of cash.

If the Boer War had stretched postal logistics to the limit, the scale of postal operations during World War I was colossal in comparison. By 1917, the British army on the Western Front was sending home over eight million letters per week via the Royal Engineers Postal Section (REPS), the successor to the Army Post Office Corps. The staff of 30 at the Mount Pleasant Sorting office in London grew to 2,540 by the end of the war, and the premises were moved to larger accommodation in Regents Park. Troops enjoyed free postage for letters under four ounces in weight, and postage from home was a penny per ounce. Letters took somewhere between 12 hours and three days to reach the Western Front from the London sorting center, depending on the location of the unit. In the field, the bare essentials of a post office were carried in a black iron box. Once the box was unloaded, a red and white flag was displayed, so troops knew they could buy stamps, purchase postal orders, etc., even if they were in the unlikely surroundings of a shed, barn, or even a trench. Postal staff in the Returned Letter Office in London were among the first to realize the extent of the casualties in the Battle of the Somme in July 1916, as huge amounts of mail were returned as undeliverable. Concerned about the effect this information would have on public morale, the government instructed postal staff to tell no one about their work.

The logistical problems thrown up by the conflicts in the many theaters of World War II simply meant that post took longer to reach its destination. The staff of the REPS sent to France with the BEF (British Expeditionary Forces) in 1940, remained absolutely committed to guarding the mail, however. In May 1940, 26,000 bags of mail were left stranded in Le Havre, but rather than abandon the letters, the Royal Engineer Postal Service mounted a guard and managed to return them to England shortly before the Dunkirk evacuation; an incredible feat given the shortage of transport for soldiers, let alone postal sacks. Once Italy entered the war in June 1940, direct air and sea links between Britain and the Middle East were severed, and planes took a circuitous route across North Africa and north over the Atlantic to Britain.

During the most bleak period of the war for Britain, 1940–1941, it was felt that the slow mail service between Britain and the Middle East was having an adverse effect on morale of the troops and their families. Bulky mail sacks used up valuable air freight space that could better be employed for troops and supplies, and the obvious solution was to reduce the weight of the mail. The introduction of the air letter—a lightweight, self-sealing letter form—immediately reduced the sheer bulk of mail sacks. Initially, they were rationed to one man per month to further preserve freight capacity.

The V-mail (known as the airgraph in Britain), was another wartime innovation and was the work of Kodak. Letters were written on preprinted forms which were then photographed on 16mm film; one film could hold 1,800 letters and weighed five ounces, which was considerably less than the sackload of mail reproduced on it. The films were flown to processing laboratories in the home country and the letters printed and sent on to the recipients through the civilian postal service. Transit time for V-mail averaged ten days. Initially popular, the British airgraph's use was limited because of its small size and the perceived lack of privacy. Postage was the same as an air letter, although use was not rationed.

It is perhaps hard for those of us accustomed to the immediacy of CNN and e-mail to recapture the intense need for news felt by the relatives of those in the front line. Families waved off their sons to battle, barely expecting to hear whether they were alive or dead until after the hostilities were over. Today, we are bombarded by news, opinion, and comment, from newspapers, radio, and television; we know what the generals look like, we read opinions of their style of leadership, and can probably watch their prosecution of the war live on television. One hundred and fifty years ago, letters filled the information void, often providing mundane details about the great and good, to satisfy the curious: "General Breckinridge is called the handsomest man in the Confederate army, and Bragg might be called the ugliest. He looks like an old porcupine," wrote one woman to her soldier husband after the generals had visited her town during the Civil War. Furthermore, in the 19th century, news took far longer to reach home. Even General Napier's pithy one-word dispatch, "*Peccavi*," which translates as "I have sinned," sent after he had captured Sind in 1843 took several days to

Above: A British soldier in Normandy writes a letter home to his father during World War II.

reach his superiors in Delhi, and then another month (via sea) to arrive in London. Even today, however, it takes a letter or e-mail to reassure relatives of an individual's safety.

The immediacy of foreign wars is a very recent phenomenon; as recently as the Falklands War, British communications with fighting troops were hampered by the shortage of satellite phones. During the 20th century, radio communication meant that the control of battle was more efficient, but the combatants themselves in the thick of the fighting, still relied on pen and paper to correspond with their families. Soldiers who became prisoners of war could communicate with their families only intermittently (transporting the letters of enemy prisoners is hardly a priority in wartime) but their families sometimes received a stark printed card with the most basic information, such as this card issued to Japanese POWs:

"I am interned in…
My health is excellent.
I am ill in hospital.
I am working for pay.
I am not working.
Please see that … is taken care of.
My love to you."

Interestingly, SAS troops were issued a similar, brusque missive, giving relatives the bare minimum of information, in the 1960s.

New technology

Samuel Morse first demonstrated his electric telegraph system in 1844, but Morse code, the system of dots and dashes, was not developed until 1867, when the Royal Navy adopted it. Both sides in the American Civil War used telegraphy, and the well-financed Union army employed a mobile field service to lay cables. Efficient communication was vital, so cutting the lines was an effective means of weakening the enemy. "Answer quick, as I know we will not have the telegraph long," wrote Sherman urgently to his superior Grant in 1864. Morse was never going to be a method of allowing soldiers to communicate with their families, but the later introduction of telegrams and cables did mean that really urgent news could be conveyed quickly. The Royal Engineers Telegraph Battalion was formed in 1870, and was attached to the 24th Middlesex Rifles, the postal company in 1883.

Today, soldiers and their families have far greater opportunities for communication. In Britain, the "Bluey" is the successor to the wartime air letter, and the airgraph has been succeeded by the "E-bluey," an e-mail

Above: A Salvation Army worker writes a letter home for a wounded soldier during World War I.

service. During the Gulf War, the "Any Service Member Mail" program was introduced in the United States, whereby whole classes of children or individuals could write to soldiers in the field and often receive informative replies, packed with details about their lives. Such letters are great morale-boosters for the soldiers, who are deployed in tricky military situations offset by even more labyrinthine political considerations. In 1999, Geraldine Lubkeman First Lieutenant and Ambulance Platoon Leader, 557th Ambulance Company wrote from Kosovo:

"I am an ambulance platoon leader in charge of ten ambulances and twenty soldiers. . . This deployment has been very difficult for us. Our job is to transport casualties to the hospital so we see every injury that occurs. Many of them are due to mine fields outside the region of our camp. . ."

She also described harrowing scenes of lives torn apart by civil war and remarked that it made her and her colleagues reflect on the true value of life.

Censorship
Today's soldiers understand the critical need for military secrecy, but 200 years ago when communications were slower, it was barely considered by soldiers writing home. During the American Revolution, both sides gained valuable information by seizing the enemy's mail. "An intercepted letter from a Gentleman of Philadelphia who has joined the Enemy... declares... that the Army would be there in Ten or Twenty days from the 16th Inst," wrote Washington from Trenton in 1776. As early as the Peninsular War, Wellington wanted letters to be censored, knowing that information about troop numbers and positions was extremely valuable to the enemy. He established a large network of spies to discover French plans, and knew that the French were keen to learn anything they could about English tactics. Letters written during the American Civil War are often remarkably frank about positions and conditions. "We had some very hard Marching and water very poor and Scarce the heat was very hard on the men we advanced with in 1 mile of Jackson and there we stopped and have been Skirmishing for the last four days yesterday evening was relieved and fell back for rest... The 46th Regt is on our right about 3 miles from here," wrote one garrulous correspondent to his parents in 1863 from Vicksburg.

By the time of World War I, all soldiers knew that their mail was censored and most chose their words carefully; they may have felt inhibited by the fact that an officer was censoring their letters, but it was one of the many facets of army life that they came to accept. The censor imposed his views all too visibly, by striking out passages deemed injurious to national security, or in some cases, delicate sensibilities. In November 1916, an official pamphlet was issued to reinforce to troops the need for discretion. Entitled *Censorship*

Orders and Regulations for Troops in the Field, it listed nine subject areas which were to be excluded from letters, including comments on the effects of enemy fire, the physical and moral condition of the troops and details of defensive works. Officers tasked with censoring the letters of their troops usually did so with discretion, although occasionally they added a "PS" of their own. "As your son's Company Officer I have to censor his letter. He has said very little about his own doings. He worked extraordinarily well and by his own example encouraged his men to hold on a the barricade for nearly 24 hours until finally relieved. It is owing to his exertions that we managed to hold our ground at that particular spot," wrote one lieutenant on his sergeant's modest letter home in 1915. Some letters did slip through the net, however. Soldiers returning home on leave during World War I often took letters from their colleagues to post in England, and others tried to send them through the French or Belgian civilian postal services.

"I have been ashore once more. I should love to tell you where but you will just have to guess I am afraid for the time-being," wrote one officer en route to Egypt in 1941. During World War II everyone, civilian or uniformed, was aware of the dangers of letting slip information to the enemy. "Loose Lips Sink Ships" and "Careless Talk Costs Lives" were the American and British poster campaigns that drummed home the dangers of indiscrete talk. Military censorship continued in much the same way as World War I, with officers censoring the letters of their men. Censoring letters was a long job, usually carried out by junior officers. Perhaps the only thing in its favor was that it enabled the officer to gauge the feelings of his men and assess their morale and state of readiness. "Have just been censoring the men's mail, and they seem happy enough," wrote one lieutenant of life on a ship. Many American troops, the sons of immigrants, wrote home in their family's mother tongue and some of their letters never made it past the censoring authorities. If the censor couldn't understand it, it was destroyed on the off chance that it risked national security.

By the time of the Korean War, censorship was phased out and letters from Vietnam flowed freely, unread by anyone except the addressees. The unhappiness, anger, and frustration evident in many letters from Vietnam would never have passed a World War II censor, as such expressions of dissatisfaction would have been deemed poor for morale.

Today, as the cameras of television crews accompany troops into battle, censoring letters would be pointless. Despite the vast improvements in communications technology, letters are still written between soldiers and their loved ones. Unlike e-mails or phone calls, they cannot disappear into the electronic ether and will remain as permanent records of the feelings and experiences of brave men and women.

A MAP

OF

NEW YORK & STATE

AND PART OF

LONG ISLA

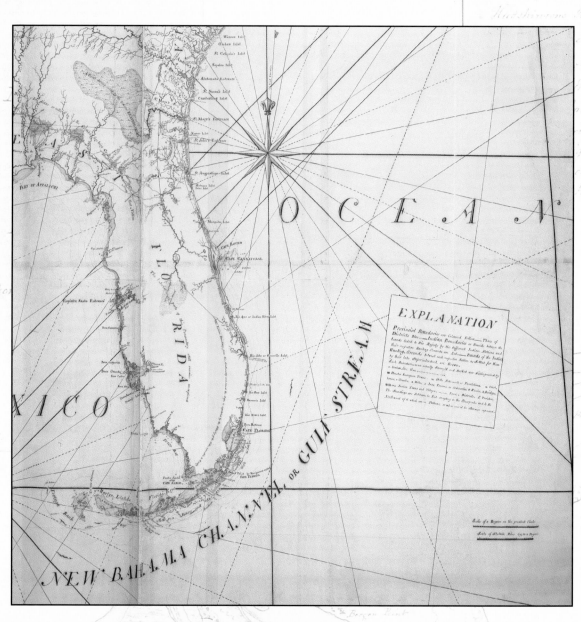

Right: Produced toward the end of the American War of Independence (1781), this map includes East and West Florida; at this time Florida was part of the British-ruled area of North America. However with the Treaty of Paris that confirmed United States independence in 1783, Florida was returned to Spanish rule.

Far right: A group of Bostonians disguised as Native Americans empty the crates of tea from three British merchant ships into Boston Harbor, as a protest against the tea tax imposed by the English on colonists. This act of defiance, known as the Boston Tea Party, was an instigating factor in the American War of Independence.

The American War of Independence 1775–1783

The American War of Independence (or the American Revolution) was fought by the colonists of America in a successful struggle to win independence from Great Britain. During the 18th century much of North America had become a battle ground as European powers sought to expand their colonial dominions. The colonies of France and Spain, as well as those of Britain, were subject to punitive trading laws that milked them of vast sums of money and kept them in a state of dependence on the "mother country." Colonists, many of whom had been born in North America, were taxed by distant governments for whom they felt little affinity, let alone allegiance. By the 1760s, the population of the 13 colonies had reached over a million and a half people, and colonial society, legislature and debate had evolved to the point where some people began to question the necessity of British dominion over them.

In popular mythology the war began with the Boston Tea Party in 1773, but for at least a decade before, the rumblings of discontent had become more insistent. The British parliament imposed a series of taxes on the wealthy colonies in an attempt to banish a domestic debt made worse by involvement in costly foreign wars. They insisted that troops stationed in North America should be quartered at the colonies' (rather than the Crown's) expense. At the heart of the colonists' discontent was the cry "no taxation without representation." They were being taxed, but as they had no vote, they had no powers of protest through the legislature.

For Britain, the war was rather different from the fighting the British army was accustomed to in Europe, as neither the landscape nor the enemy leant themselves to the usual set-piece battles. They faced guerrilla fighters, who not only lacked formal uniforms, but wore trappers' clothes that blended into the landscape. The British Red Coats were far more conspicuous in comparison and also constrained by the formal methods of fighting and drilling.

The colonies had always possessed militia companies, formed initially to protect the small towns and communities from Indian incursions. By the

1760s, the annual musters became little more than social events, however, and the military skills of the militias declined. In October 1774, the Americans reorganized the militia, allocating a quarter of their best troops to companies of "minute men" who were formed up and ready for action at a moment's notice. With a lack of experienced commanders, however, the chain of command was weak, and discipline was often poor.

The British government had very little direct control over events, separated as they were from the action by 3,000 miles of ocean and at least two month's traveling time. This great distance exacerbated supply and logistics problems too. Although a sizeable portion of the British forces was made up of loyal colonists, professional soldiers and munitions had to be shipped from Britain. Nevertheless, they were the superior force, and to begin with, inflicted a series of losses on the colonial troops.

In 1773, 3,000 troops were sent to Massachusetts from Britain under Major General Thomas Gage to join those already there. Gage, the governor of Massachusetts struggled to keep the peace between his bored soldiery and the increasingly disgruntled colonists, but the colonists were preparing to oppose their colonial masters and Gage's clumsy patrols could do little to stop them. The first shots of the war were fired in Lexington in 1775, when a force of 700 men, including the 10th Regiment of Foot under Lieutenant Colonel Francis Smith, was dispatched from Boston to confiscate arms and equipment from colonial forces. They were met by a force of 150 militia, who, seeing they were outnumbered, retreated. Firing broke out almost by accident while the British were destroying the few supplies and munitions they could find. Smith's report to his commanding officer, General Gage, is both businesslike and astute. He emphasizes that the British did not intend to hurt the colonists and was surprised by the speed with which the colonial forces assembled. He seems irked that they merely harassed his troops, and would perhaps have preferred a "proper" engagement.

"In obedience to your Excellency's commands, I marched on the evening of the 18th inst. with the corps of grenadiers and light infantry for Concord, to execute your Excellency's orders with respect to destroying all ammunition, artillery, tents, &c., collected there, which was effected, having knocked off the trunnions of three pieces of iron ordnance, some new gun carriages, a great number of carriage wheels burnt, a considerable quantity of flour, some gunpowder and musket balls, with other small articles thrown into the river. Notwithstanding we marched with the utmost expedition and

secrecy, we found the country had intelligence or strong suspicion of our coming, and fired many signal guns, and rung the alarm bells repeatedly; and were informed, when at Concord, that some cannon had been taken out of the town that day, that others, with some stores, had been carried three days before...

While at Concord we saw vast numbers assembling in many parts; at one of the bridges they marched down, with a very considerable body, on the light infantry posted there. On their coming pretty near, one of our men fired on them, which they returned; on which an action ensued, and some few were killed and wounded. In this affair, it appears that after the bridge was quitted, they scalped and otherwise ill-treated one or two of the men who were either killed or severely wounded, being seen by a party that marched by soon after. At Concord we found very few inhabitants in the town; those we met with both Major Pitcairn and myself took all possible pains to convince that we meant them no injury, and that if they opened their doors when required to search for military stores, not the slightest mischief would be done. We had opportunities of convincing them of our good intentions, but they were sulky; and one of them even struck Major Pitcairn.

On our leaving Concord to return to Boston, they began to fire on us from behind the walls, ditches, trees, etc., which, as we marched, increased to a very great degree, and continued without the intermission of five minutes altogether, for, I believe, upwards of eighteen miles; so that I can't think but it must have been a preconcerted scheme in them, to attack the King's troops the first favourable opportunity that offered, otherwise, I think they could not, in so short a time as from our marching out, have raised such a numerous body, and for so great a space of ground. Notwithstanding the enemy's numbers, they did not make one gallant effort during so long an action, though our men were so very much fatigued, but kept under cover"

Right: A romanticized image of American patriot Paul Revere who rode from Boston to Concord, warning of the approach of British troops. His news enabled the colonists to hide their equipment from the British.

Smith believed that the colonists had "strong suspicion of our coming" and he was right. They had been alerted to the approach of the British on April 18 by one Paul Revere, on his romanticized "Midnight Ride" from Charlestown to Lexington, Massachusetts, a distance of some 15 miles. An accomplished silversmith, Revere was one of the original "Sons of Liberty" who organized popular resistance to the Stamp Act and the Boston Massacre. He was also an excellent horseman and acted as a courier, ferrying messages between colonial leaders. On April 15, he noticed that British troops in Boston were being prepared for action, along with ships of the Royal Navy, and reported his observations to Dr. Warren of the colonial Committee of Safety. His mad dash by horseback to Lexington forewarned the colonial leaders John Hancock and Sam Adams, giving them enough time to conceal or remove the munitions. Revere rode on to Concord, where he was arrested and questioned by the British. He was released, but his horse was confiscated and the only way back was on foot. When his wife Rachel learned of his plight she tried to send him £125 (about $180) via a trusted third party, Dr. Benjamin Church. Although Church appeared to be an upright citizen of the colonial community—he was a member of the Massachusetts Provincial Congress and surgeon to Washington's troops—he was also a spy for the British, reporting troop movements and British plans direct to General Gage. Rachel's letter never reached her husband and nor, needless to say, did the money, which was a huge sum by the standards of the time (the equivalent of about $13,000 today).

"My Dear by Doctor Church I send a hundred & twenty five pounds and beg you will take the best care of yourself and not attempt coming in to this town again and if I have an opportunity of coming or sending out anything or any of the Children I shall do it pray keep up your spirits and trust your self and us in the hands of a good God who will take care of us tis all my Dependance for vain is the help of man adieu my Love from your affectionate R. Revere"

If the British were surprised by the colonial opposition at Lexington and Concord, the arrival of 20,000 colonial militia outside Boston horrified them. The Massachusetts Congress called it the "Army of Observation," but these troops effectively besieged Boston. At the end of May, troops and supplies arrived from Britain while the colonial Committee of Safety resolved to tighten their grip on Boston. The resulting battle of Bunker Hill (actually fought on Breed's Hill in Boston) dislodged the rebels from their advanced positions, but did not break the siege. The British sustained heavy casualties, with 42 percent of their 2,500-strong force killed or injured. The following letter was written five days after the battle by Lieutenant J. Waller of the First Royal Marine Battalion to his brother, and his breathless prose captures the struggle perfectly.

"Camp of Charlestown Heights, 22 June 1775

Amidst the hurry and confusion of a camp hastily pitched in the field of battle, I am sat down to tell you I have escaped unhurt, where many, very many, have fallen. The public papers will inform you of the situation of the ground and the redoubt that we attacked on the heights of Charlestown. I can only say that it was a most desperate and daring attempt, and it was performed with as much gallantry and spirit as was ever shown by any troops in any age.

Two companies of the first battalion of Marines, and part of the 47th Regiment, were the first that mounted the breast-work: and you will not be displeased when I tell you that I was with those two companies, who drove their bayonets into all that opposed them. Nothing could be more shocking than the carnage that followed the storming this work. We tumbled over the dead to get at the living, who were crowding out of the gorge of the redoubt, in order to form under the defences which they had prepared to cover their retreat. In these breast-works they had artillery, which did so much mischief; but these they were obliged to abandon, being followed closely by the Light Infantry, who suffered exceedingly in the pursuit. The rebels had 5000 to 7000 men, covered by a redoubt, breast-works, walls, hedges, trees and the like; and the number of the corps under General Howe, (who performed this gallant business) did not amount to 1500. We gained a complete victory, and entrenched ourselves that night, where we lay under arms, in the front of the field of battle. We lay the next night on the ground, and the following day encamped. The officers have not their marquees, but are obliged to lie in soldier's tents, they being more portable in case of our advancing.

We had of our corps one major, 2 captains, and 3 lieutenants killed; 4 captains and 3 lieutenants wounded; 2 serjeants and 21 rank and file killed, and 3 serjeants and 79 privates wounded; and I suppose, upon the whole, we lost, killed and wounded, from 800 to

1000 men. We killed a number of the rebels, but the cover they fought under made their loss less considerable than it would otherwise have been. The army is in great spirits, and full of rage and ferocity at the rebellious rascals, who both poisoned and chewed the musket balls, in order to make them the more fatal. Many officers have died of their wounds, and others very ill: 'tis astonishing what a number of officers were hit on this occasion; but the officers were particularly aimed at.

I will just give you a short account of the part of the action where I was particularly concerned. We landed close under Charlestown, and formed with the 47th Regiment close under the natural defences of the redoubt, which we drove the enemy from, climbing over rails and hedges. So we closed upon them; but when we came immediately under the work, we were checked by the severe fire of the enemy, but did not retreat an inch. We were now in confusion, after being broke several times in getting over the rails, etc. I did all I could to form the two companies on our right, which at last I effected, losing many of them while it was performing. Major Pitcairne was killed close by me, with a captain and a subaltern, also a serjeant, and many of the privates; and had we stopped there much longer, the enemy would have picked us all off.

I saw this, and begged Colonel Nesbitt of the 47th to form on our left, in order that we might advance with our bayonets to the parapet. I ran from right to left, and stopped our men from firing; while this was doing, and when we had got in tolerable order, we rushed on, leaped the ditch, and climbed the parapet, under a most sore and heavy fire. Colonel Nesbitt spoke very favourably of my conduct, and both our Majors have mentioned me to Lord Sandwich in consequence of it. One captain and one subaltern fell in getting up, and one captain and one subaltern was wounded of our corps; three captains of the 52nd were killed on the parapet, and others that I know nothing of. God bless you! I did not think, at one time, that I should ever have been able to write this, though in the heat of the action I thought nothing of the matter."

Waller's letter remarks on several of the American methods that became commonplace throughout the war. They aimed their fire particularly at the British officers and remained under cover as far as possible to minimize risk to themselves.

While this battle was going on, the Second Continental Congress was meeting in Philadelphia to formally appoint a competent general. On July 3, 1775, George Washington arrived to take control of the American troops. Washington was a professional soldier who had fought bravely in the French and Indian wars 20 years earlier. He set about training the 14,000 troops and recruiting more from both the colonists and the Native Americans. His letters repeatedly bemoan his lack of supplies and men, especially "powder" for the guns, but he managed to struggle against these obstacles to produce a proficient army.

"To Major General Philip Schuyler, August 14, 1775
Cambridge Camp, August 14, 1775

Sir: I received your Favour of the 31st July informing me of your Preparations to cross the Lake, and inclosing the Affidavits of John Shatforth and John Duguid. Several Indians of the Tribe of St. Francis came in here Yesterday and confirm the former Accounts of the good Dispositions of the Indian Nations, and Canadians to the Interests of America. A most happy Event, on which I sincerely congratulate you. (Yesterday Sen-night arrived at the camp in Cambridge, Swashan, the Chief, with four other Indians of the St. Francois tribe, conducted thither by Mr. Reuben Colburn, who has been honorably recompensed for his trouble. The above Indians came hither to offer their service in the cause of American liberty, have been kindly received, and are now entered into service. Swashan says he will bring one half of his tribe and has engaged 4 or 5 other tribes if they should be wanted. He says the Indians of Canada in general, and also the French, are greatly in our favor, and determined not to act against us.

I am glad to relieve you from your Anxiety, respecting Troops being sent from Boston to Quebeck. These Reports, I apprehend, took their Rise from a Fleet being fitted about fourteen Days ago to plunder the islands in the Sound, of their live Stock; an Expedition which they have executed with some Success, and are just returning; but you may depend on it no Troops have been detached from Boston for Canada or elsewhere. Among other Wants, of which, I find you have your Proportion, we feel that of Lead most sensibly, and as we have no Expectation of a Supply from the Southward, I have concluded to draw up on the Stock found at Ticonderoga, when it fell into our Hands. I am informed, it is considerable, and a Part of it may be spared, without exposing you to any Inconvenience. In Consequence of this I have wrote to Governor Trumbull, to take the Direction of the Transportation of it, supposing the Conveyance through Connecticut the most safe and expeditious. I expect he will write you on this Subject by this Opportunity.

I have nothing new, my dear Sir, to write you. We are precisely in the same Situation as to Enemy, as when I wrote you last, nor can I gain any certain Intelligence of their future Intentions. The Troops from the Southward are come in very healthy and in good Order. Tomorrow I expect a Supply of Powder from Philadelphia, which will be a most seasonable Relief in our present Necessity.

God grant you Health and Success equal to your Merit and Wishes. – Favour me with Intelligence as often as you can, and believe me with very sincere Regard. Dear Sir, Yours, &c.

Go. Washington"

Washington forced the British to evacuate Boston in March 1776 after a miserable winter during which both sides had suffered from a shortage of supplies and food. He placed great store by having a well-behaved army, as his "Order on Profanity" published on August 3, 1776, shows:

"...That the Troops may have an opportunity of attending public worship, as well as take some rest after the great fatigue they have gone through; The General in future excuses them from fatigue duty on Sundays (except at the Ship Yards, or special occasions) until further orders. The General is sorry to be informed that the foolish, and wicked practice, of profane cursing and swearing (a Vice heretofore little known in an American Army) is growing into fashion; he hopes the officers will, by example, as well as influence, endeavour to check it, and that both they, and the men will reflect, that we can have little hopes of the blessing of Heaven on our Arms, if we insult it by our impiety, and folly; added to this, it is a vice so mean and low, without any temptation, that every man of sense, and character, detests and despises it."

Washington moved on to New York, where he was beaten at the battle of Brooklyn Heights. Retreating demoralized, he revived American morale by his surprise attack on British forces at Trenton on Christmas Day 1776. This letter, written the day before the attack, gives little cause for optimism. Washington is plagued by deserting troops, problems of appointing decent officers, and a shortage of money to pay the army. Furthermore, he is worried that his army is outnumbered by the British under Howe, who was threatening the capital, Philadelphia. In the light of these problems, Washington's victory the next day at Trenton seems all the more remarkable. He captured more than 900 Hessian troops in the service of the British, as well as sorely needed stores and supplies. American morale soared.

"Camp above Trenton falls
Decr. 24th 1776

Sir,

That I should dwell upon the subject of our distresses cannot be more disagreeable to Congress than it is painful to myself. The alarming situation to which our Affairs are reduced, impels me to the measure.

Inquiry and investigation which in most cases serve to devellope and point out a remedy, in ours, present more and greater difficulties.

'till of late I was led to hope from reports, that no inconsiderable part of the troops composing the Regiments that were with Genl. Lee and those from Ticonderoga under Genl. Gates, had enlisted again.

This intelligence I confess gave me reason to expect that I should have at the expiration of the present year, a force some what more respectable than what I find will be the case: having examined into the state of those Regiments, I am authorized to say from the information of their Officers, that but very few of the men have inlisted.

Right: A map of New York and Staten Island, 1776–1782. Major General Howe intended to capture New York in 1776, but Washington defended the city with a series of rearguard actions on Manhattan Island from August to November. Howe eventually drove the colonists out across New Jersey and into Pennsylvania.

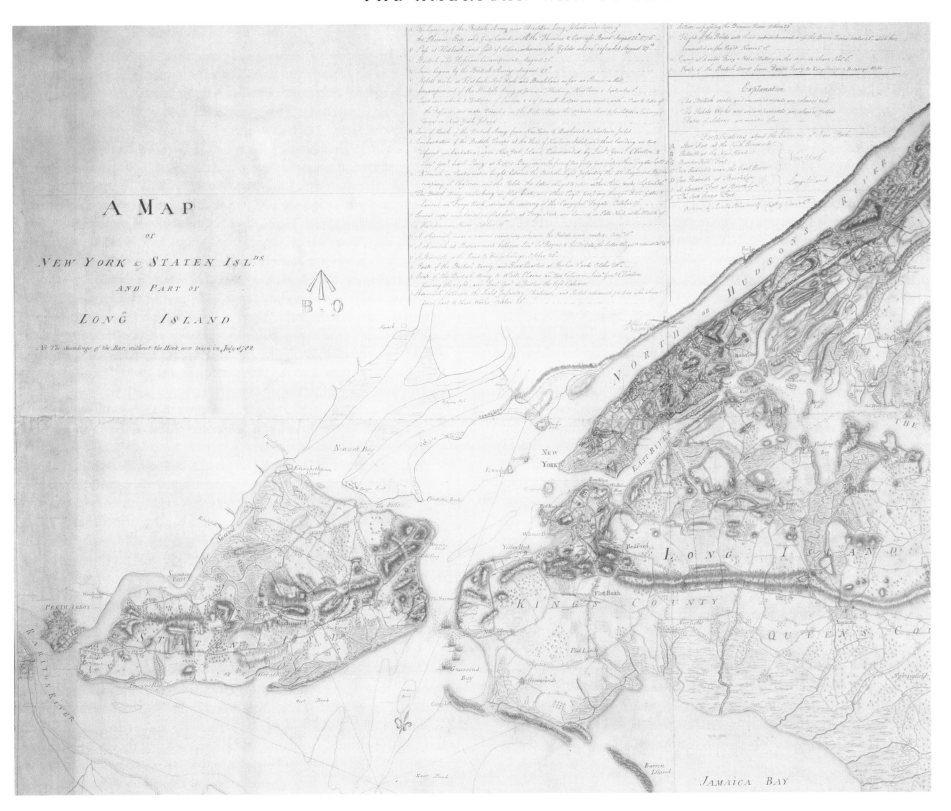

A MAP

OF

NEW YORK & STATEN ISL.DS

AND PART OF

LONG ISLAND

heed forming'; we rushed on amidst the heaviest fire I have yet felt. It was no longer a contest for bringing up our respective companies in the best order, but all officers as well as soldiers strove who could be foremost, to my shame I speak it. I had the fortune to find myself after crossing the swamp with three officers only, in the midst of a large body of Rebels who had been driven out of the wood by the 1st Battalion of Grenadiers, accompanied by not more than a dozen men who had been able to keep up with us; luckily the Rebels were too intent on their own safety to regard our destruction.

The column which we routed in this disorderly manner consisted of 4000, the force on our side not more than 800. In the mean time the pursuit of this column brought us on their main Army led by Washington, said by deserters to be 16,000. With some difficulty we were brought under the hill we had gained, and the most terrible cannonade ensued and lasted for above two hours, at the distance of 600 yards. The shattered remains of our Battalion being under cover of our hill suffered little, but from thirst and heat of which several died, except some who preferred the shade of some trees in the direct range of shot to the more horrid tortures of thirst."

In the days before army medicals, soldiers paraded in varying states of physical fitness. George Washington, a wealthy man, was probably in better shape than many of his soldiers, but the following letter illustrates the problems he had with his famous false teeth. More importantly, the letter was captured by the British before it reached its destination and may have helped the British ascertain Washington's whereabouts at a time when stealth and surprise were critical to the colonists' military campaigning.

Below: Generals Rochambeau and Washington give the last orders for attack at the siege of Yorktown, 1781. With them is the Marquis de Lafayette.

"New Windsor May 29, 1781

Sir,
A day or two ago I requested Col. Harrison to apply to you for a pair of Pincers to fasten the wire of my teeth.

I hope you furnished him with them. I now wish you would send me one of your scrapers as my teeth stand in need of cleaning, and I have little prospect of being in Philadelphia soon. It will come very safe by the Post & in return, the money shall be sent so soon as I know the cost of it.

I am Sir
Y Very H Serv [Your Very Humble Servant]

G. Washington"

In 1778, Sir Henry Clinton took over as British commander in chief to replace Howe. He was directed to concentrate his forces against New York and to send troops and ships to guard British Caribbean possession from the French. Britain enjoyed a series of successes in the south, particularly along the coast where they could coordinate land and sea forces. But the hinterland was far harder to pacify, and the British faced tenacious rebel guerrillas who continued to outsmart them. Major General Nathanael Greene assembled a new American army and coordinated his movements with the guerrilla units to unsettle the more numerous British under Lord Cornwallis. Finally, in October 1781, having isolated almost every enemy post from Georgia to Virginia, Greene pinned down Cornwallis and his army at Yorktown.

In eight years of fighting, over 60,000 British soldiers had been sent across the Atlantic to tackle the colonists, whose determination had been harnessed by Washington and his generals to ensure their victory.

Below: The Independence Hall of Philadelphia, Pennsylvania, was where the United States Constitution was written, the Declaration of Independence was first read, and the Liberty Bell was rung to proclaim its adoption.

Right: Detail of a map that shows the frontiers of France, Britain, and their neighboring countries following the Treaties of Versailles, Amiens, Tilsit, and Pressburg, from 1783–1807.

Far right: Arthur Wellesley. Duke of Wellington, known to his troops as the "Iron Duke," or "Nosey," was Commander of the British Army from 1809 to 1815.

The Napoleonic Wars 1792–1815

Strictly speaking the wars between France and Britain at the turn of the 18th/19th century should be split in two. The Revolutionary War fought between the Republic of France and Britain began in 1792. In 1799, Napoleon became Consul of France for life and effectively ended the French Revolution. By 1804 he had crowned himself Emperor. After 1799 the Napoleonic Wars began and lasted until the French defeat at the battle of Waterloo in June 1815.

The whole of Europe was embroiled in war. Battles were fought from Russia through Austria, Italy, Spain, Portugal, and France as Napoleon extended his empire to embrace the whole continent. Fighting extended to India, the West Indies, and even America, as Britain sought to preserve her colonies from French incursion, or better still, acquire French territories.

Both sides could call upon a spectacular array of military and naval talent. Napoleon, Nelson, and Wellington immediately spring to mind, but they were supported by officers such as Ney, Masséna, Davout, Archduke Charles, Moore, Napier, Crauford, Howe, Jervis, and Beresford. "I only hope that when the enemy reads the list of their names, he trembles as I do" remarked Wellington in August 1810 (echoing the words of Lord Chesterfield a century earlier). Napoleon was undefeated in Europe for several years. Between 1800 and 1809 his string of victories—Ulm, Marengo, and Austerlitz among them—stand as a memorial to his great military talent and the fighting of the Grand Armée. Only the British prevented his complete domination, defeating him at sea in Egypt in 1799 and at Trafalgar in 1805.

By 1807, Napoleon had forced Prussia, Austria, and Russia to humiliating defeat and turned his attention to Portugal, invading partly to halt British trade. With his brother Joseph installed as King of Spain in 1808, Napoleon had reckoned without a full-scale revolt against the French, and the intervention of the British to support it. The Peninsular Campaign began in 1808. Sir Arthur Wellesley (later the Duke of Wellington) arrived from Portugal to take command in 1809 after the

original commander, Sir John Moore, died. It took Wellington five years using a combined force of British, Portuguese, and Spanish troops to drive the French back across the Pyrenées.

Arguably, Napoleon overextended himself. Despite the fact that fighting in the Peninsula was not going well, in 1812 he invaded Russia with a force of over 450,000 troops and 1,400 guns, an immense army by any standards. The Russians retreated and stood against the French at Borodino, 75 miles west of Moscow, where both sides suffered serious losses. Napoleon entered Moscow, but the Russians burned large parts of the city and, faced with the impenetrable cold of the Russian winter, Napoleon withdrew slowly across the Steppes. The Grand Armée was devastated by hunger, exhaustion, disease, and cold and only ten percent of the troops survived.

In 1813, Wellington had driven the French from Spain and Portugal, and the remnants of the Grand Armée were limping home. Although opposed by most of Europe (Britain, Prussia, Russia, Austria, and Sweden formed the Sixth Coalition) Napoleon managed to form a new army and was able to fight the Allies at Leipzig until he retreated with his army intact in October 1813. In 1814, France was invaded, but Napoleon continued to fight off the invaders until, on March 31, Paris was captured. Napoleon abdicated a week later and was exiled to the island of Elba. That should have been the end of the story, but on March 1, 1815, the Emperor returned to France, capitalizing on dissatisfaction with the restored Bourbon King Louis XVIII. He received a hero's welcome and returned to Paris on March 20 to the abject horror of the allies who were meeting at the Congress of Vienna to discuss European reconstruction. Napoleon decided to preempt another allied invasion of France by sending an army to Belgium to tackle the Prussian and Anglo-Dutch forces separately. Incredibly, he was successful until June 18, 1815, when he faced Wellington at Waterloo.

Below: In June 1812, Napoleon launched an army of nearly half a million men on Russia. By the time they reached Smolensk in August, 75,000 had perished, most from disease. After the Battle of Borodino on September 7, the French lost another 30,000 men, leaving an exhausted force of 95,000 men to enter Moscow.

During the Revolutionary Wars, Britain rarely engaged French forces on land, concentrating instead on using naval power to end French dreams of either invading Britain, or of establishing an eastern empire to rival British possessions in India. The Royal Navy sustained and protected Britain's commercial and military strength and Nelson's outstanding victory at Trafalgar destroyed the threat of a French invasion.

Horatio Nelson was undoubtedly an exceptional naval tactician, and his professional letters and dispatches reveal an economy and clarity of words vital to successful military communication. According to contemporaries, however, he was also an unusually vain man, and his private letters to his mistress Lady Hamilton reveal yet another side of the great admiral.

In 1798, the French set out to conquer Egypt and block the British overland route to India. As the French entered Cairo in August 1798, Nelson's fleet entered Aboukir Bay to find the French fleet at anchor, an opportunity that was too good to miss. Nelson destroyed the French ships, leaving Napoleon's troops stranded in Egypt. His subsequent report to the Admiralty is both businesslike and generous in its praise of his officers.

"Vanguard, off the Mouth of the Nile, 3 August 1798

My Lord,

Almighty God has blessed His Majesty's Arms in the late Battle, by a great Victory over the Fleet of the Enemy, who I attacked at sunset on the 1st of August, off the Mouth of the Nile. The Enemy were moored in a strong Line of Battle for defending the entrance of the Bay, (of Shoals,) flanked by numerous Gun-boats, four Frigates, and a Battery of Guns and Mortars on an Island in their Van; but nothing could withstand the Squadron your Lordship did me the honour to place under my command. Their high state of discipline is well known to you, and with the judgment of the Captains, together with their valour, and that of the Officers and Men of every description, it was absolutely irresistible. Could anything from my pen add to the character of the Captains, I would write it with pleasure, but that is impossible.

I have to regret the loss of Captain Westcott of the Majestic, who was killed early in the Action; but the Ship was continued to be so well fought by her First Lieutenant, Mr. Cuthbert, that I have given him an order to command her till your Lordship's pleasure is known.

Above: Boys as young as nine could be recruited to join the Navy. Sir John Ross, the noted Arctic explorer, joined the Navy at this tender age in 1786 and served during the Napoleonic Wars with distinction.

Above: Lady Hamilton as "Nature" by George Romney

Above: Portrait of Horatio Nelson by Leonardo Guzzardi

The Ships of the Enemy, all but their two rear Ships, are nearly dismasted: and those two, with two Frigates, I am sorry to say, made their escape; nor was it, I assure you, in my power to prevent them. Captain Hood most handsomely endeavoured to do it, but I had no Ship in a condition to support the Zealous, and I was obliged to call her in.

The support and assistance I have received from Captain Berry cannot be sufficiently expressed. I was wounded in the head, and obliged to be carried off the deck; but the service suffered no loss by that event: Captain Berry was fully equal to the important service then going on, and to him I must beg leave to refer you for every information relative to this Victory. He will present you with the Flag of the Second in Command, that of the Commander-in-Chief being burnt in L'Orient.

Herewith I transmit you Lists of the Killed and Wounded, and the Lines of Battle of ourselves and the French. I have the honour to be, my Lord, your Lordship's most obedient Servant…"

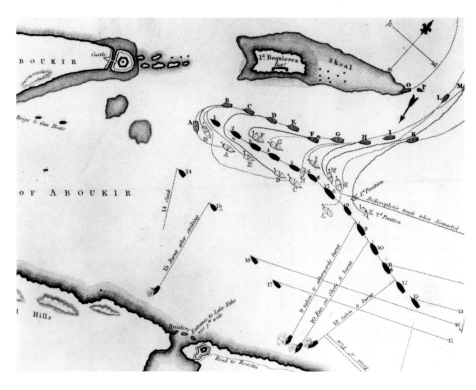

Above: Plan of the Battle of the Nile showing the position of the French and British fleets.

Left: Warships in Aboukir Bay during the Battle of the Nile.

Seven years later Nelson fought his finest and final battle at Trafalgar. His last letters to Emma Hamilton and their daughter Horatia are made more touching (like so many letters in this book) with the benefit of hindsight.

"Victory, October 19th, 1805.

My dearest Angel, I was made happy by the pleasure of receiving your letter of September 19th, and I rejoice to hear that you are so very good a girl, and love my dear Lady Hamilton, who most dearly loves you. Give her a kiss for me. The Combined Fleets of the Enemy are now reported to be coming out of Cadiz; and therefore I answer your letter, my dearest Horatia, to mark to you that you are ever uppermost in my thoughts. I shall be sure of your prayers for my safety, conquest, and speedy return to dear Merton, and our dearest good Lady Hamilton. Be a good girl, mind what Miss Connor says to you. Receive, my dearest Horatia, the affectionate parental blessing of your Father,

Nelson and Bronte"

"Victory, October 19th, 1805, Noon, Cadiz, E.S.E., 16 Leagues.

My dearest beloved Emma, the dear friend of my bosom. The signal has been made that the Enemy's Combined Fleet are coming out of Port. We have very little wind, so that I have no hopes of seeing them before to-morrow. May the God of Battles crown my endeavours with success; at all events, I will take care that my name shall ever be most dear to you and Horatia, both of whom I love as much as my own life. And as my last writing before the Battle will be to you, so I hope in God that I shall live to finish my letter after the Battle. May Heaven bless you prays your

Nelson and Bronte."

Left: Nelson's flagship *Vanguard* at the head of the British fleet, signal flags flying, faces the French at the Battle of the Nile.

Above: The death of Horatio Nelson during the Battle of Trafalgar, 1805.

Below: The Battle of Trafalgar was fought just off the Spanish coast near Cadiz.

Above: Raphael de Riego y Nunez (1785–1823), a Spanish general and revolutionary. Imprisoned by the French in 1808, he returned to Spain in 1814.

The surviving letters of the period are remarkable when compared to those of later wars by the sheer amount of military information contained within them. The writers note down their position, replay the battles almost shot by shot, report the losses and troop numbers, and comment on their commanders. All this information would have been useful to the enemy, but censorship was unknown in this period. Many soldiers complained bitterly about the conditions they lived in and Wellington, plagued by the problems of "croakers" during the Peninsular Campaign—the term for defeatist talk —suggested censoring letters. Officers and their families were expected to exercise "discretion" in passing on details from the front, but could not

always be relied upon to do so. More problematic were the consequences if letters fell into the enemies' hands. Wellington believed that men should get on with job of fighting "instead of writing such news and keeping coffee houses. But as soon as an accident happens, every man who can write, and who has a friend who can read, sits down to write his account of what he does not know."

This letter from Major Daniel Gardener to his nephew William Freer, a 19-year-old subaltern, is full of useful information about enemy movements as well as more practical advice. Rather than prepare himself with a sharp saber to face the French, William is advised to procure a mule, food, wine, and cooking pots.

"Zarza Maior, July 5 1809.

My dear William,
I hope very soon to shake you by the hand and my friend Wells also. Tell him I have received both his and your letters from England and replied to the former. The news here to-day is that the French are waiting for us at Talavera-del Reyna, that Joseph Bonaparte has joined Victor at that place with 4,000 men from Madrid. That the French Army at Talavera is consequently about 45,000, that NE, Soult and Kellerman are each moving their Divisions to form a junction. Our combined army when assembled and united will be English about 24,000 Spaniards upwards of 48,000 effective. Thus we may expect much fighting in a short time. I should imagine that your Officers are ill provided with Animals to carry Baggage etc., and I would recommend to lose no opportunity of securing any they may meet with without being too nice as to the price, as not a mule can be provided here—indeed nothing but bread and onions can be had. We have had no wine for 3 days, except a little which an officer gave us as he passed, even for the little we occasionally have found we have sent two leagues for. I lament I could not hear when you arrived at Lisbon, as I wished to have given to you some portable cooking utensils which I had made when I expected to have joined you last year... Provide yourself with everything you can at Abrante and Castel Branco as nothing can possibly be had after. Bring plenty of tea and chocolate soap and sugar. I am devillish busy, we march at 3 o'clock to-morrow morning towards Coria-Adieu God bless you. D. Gardner"

William was a couple of day's march behind his uncle, so presumably received this letter reasonably quickly, but letters from the Peninsula took at least a couple of weeks to reach Britain, traveling first though the army's supply chain before being put on a ship back to a British port, and replies arrived in an equally haphazard fashion. Major William Warre, a prolific letter writer during his service under Wellington complained:

> "I have been most truly vexed at not receiving your very affectionate letters of 5th July and 2nd August, annexed with my dear mother's of 10th July, till yesterday, late in the evening. The stupid clerks in the army post-office sent them up to Lord Wellington's army. I have for some time past been very fidgety at not hearing, and the three last packets do not bring me a line from anyone, or they also are gone to the English army while I am in Lisbon. I am sorry my letter was so expensive. It was Col. Brown's brother's fault, who told me it would go free."

Warre was writing from Lisbon on September 11, 1809, so the mail was taking between six weeks and two months to reach him. A weekly ship from Falmouth to Lisbon delivered both official mail and private correspondence. Private letters were passed to the Quartermaster-General, who had two sergeant postmasters to see that letters reached their recipients.

On the Continent at least, battles were not isolated events: armies had to be provisioned with food, horses, and accommodation, and in the case of the French army, this meant foraging from the surrounding locality. The British used commissary supply trains to supply their troops, so the British soldier was always guaranteed food, if of a rather boring and predictable nature. The usual ration was 1.5lb of bread, and 3/4lb of beef bone. British soldiers were banned from foraging, but the commissary supplies were invariably late or held up elsewhere. John Kincaid noted in his *Adventures in the Rifle Brigade*:

> "During the whole of our advance from the frontiers of Portugal, until we entered the Pyrenees, not more (on the average) than one biscuit per day was served out to each man—and it consequently could not be expected that a soldier, weighed down by a heavy knapsack, and from sixty to eighty rounds of ammunition (stick as we

Riflemen carried at the time), could march from twenty to thirty miles a day on so short an allowance.

> It was not unfrequent, therefore, after a day's march to observe groups of our regiment, and, indeed, of the division, rooting up the fields with their swords and bayonets, in search of potatoes, &c., and these were the men who were able to undergo the fatigue of the next day. The French, also, in their hurried retreat stocked themselves with several days provisions in advance; these were hung very temptingly from their knapsacks, and as it were, in defiance of our hungry jaws; as a consequence, this gave rise to the well-known remark, or alternatives of the Light Division: Damme, boys, if the Commissary don't show his front we must either find a potato field or have a killing day!"

Life as a soldier in Wellington's army was often far from comfortable. George Simmons, a British rifleman wrote to his parents February 28, 1810: "The only thing I want at present is a supply of clothes. The lying out at night in the fields for months together soon puts your raiment in disorder, I am nearly in rags."

The Freer family had three sons in the army during the Peninsular War: William, Edward, and John. William and Edward served with the 43rd, a regiment of the Light Brigade and were protégés of Sir William Napier (who wrote the classic work, *History of the War in the Peninsula and in the South of France*). It is clear from their many letters to their family in Dublin and Rutland that they were brave and able young officers. Their letters are full of hope, patriotism, and a desire to do their duty and their tone never wavers from this even when Edward and William are wounded. They took part in the brutal siege of Badajoz between March 17 and April 6, 1811, and wrote to their father a week after the battle. Their account of their wounds is typically stoical, but the sheer pain of reasonably serious injuries and the potential danger of life-threatening blood poisoning in the days before antiseptics was severe.

> "You will, by this time have heard that William and myself are wounded as Major Duffy wrote to Major Wells' Brother to inform you of the circumstance. I should have wrote also but did not know of the Post going so soon as it did. William has lost his right arm but

is getting on famously and intends writing you a few lines with his left. I am wounded through the testicles but it has not done my parts any material damage, so that I am in hopes of a speedy recovery, we have been here these last four Days but expect soon to be removed to Elvas. The Division marched on the 12th April for the North, where it is supposed Marmont is carrying operations against Ciudad Rodrigo, several other Divisions have also marched that road by forced marches. We have had extreme hard work during the Siege having had six hours work in the trenches every Day at our first commencement we had incessant rain for about five or six days which annoyed us very much, but which our Soldiers bore with their usual fortitude. I was one who had the Honour of breaking Ground. The enemy didt.[sic] find us out till the next morning.

Our Regt. have suffered most severely in the storm, having lost Eighteen Officers killed or wounded and three hundred and forty men, amongst the former our Colonel was killed, a young man loved by the whole Regt. whose loss will be much felt in the Regt. The attack began at ten o'Clock on the night of the 7th ins. We were up on the Breach for near an hour and half exposed to a most tremendous fire of musketry, hand grenades, shells, fire Balls and large stones which they threw down upon us from the Ramparts, and it was not till the fifth and third Divisions had escalated in other parts, that we could enter. Nearly every Regt. have suffered in the same proportion with our own.

Major Wells is wounded and here with us, we are ten in one House but have every accommodation we can wish for. We are attended once a day by the surgeon, who dresses our wounds. Our time passes very slow but we get over it as well as we can with the assistance of Books but which we find rather scarce, having nearly finished our stock. Capel makes one of us, he is wounded in the arm I hope to see Thomas appointed to some Regt. this Volunteering. I intend writing to my Mother by the same Packet with this. 21st April. We have been waiting an opportunity to forward this till now. We are both much recovered. Remember me to all Friends and believe me your ever dutiful Son, Edwd. G. Freer."

At the end of this letter, another begins, written by William, who had lost an arm. The handwriting is shaky and slants backward.

"My dear Father,

I hope the supposed neglect which you must of course impute to us will not hurt your feelings—the cause of you not hearing from us at the time the Dispatches were sent off was owing to their not giving us time at the Hospital to have letters [illegible]. Major Duffy however wrote to Wells in London to announce it to you. Thank God we are both doing as well as the nature of our Wounds can possibly admit of. My right arm was amputated having had a Musquet Shot which shattered it above the Elbow. I also had a slug in my backside which worked out the other night: from this place I have no pain. It is healing up. I have also a bruise on the knee from a stone with which they saluted us in the breach. A short time will bring me completely round, be assured we will not fail giving you an account of how we get on from time to time and with prayer for safety believe me my dear Father

Your affectionate Son
W. Freer."

In September 1809 Major William Warre wrote to his mother from Lisbon, obviously bored with the situation and anxious to see some action.

"You wish to know my situation in the country, etc., etc. It is simply this, I have the rank of Major, but neither pay, nor allowances, or fixed regiment. It was intended to have given those who chose it the Portuguese pay, that is those who got no rank, by entering it, in their own service. This I refused, and have already informed you of my reasons, which I hope you approve. However, since I find we are not to get it, as we receive English staff pay, and Batt and Forage, I received the other day, which, however, they threaten to make me refund, (150 f. for horses), and besides this I neither have nor do receive one farthing from their Government, or any besides my English pay.

I could indeed make it out very well on my Staff pay, but for my losses in horses. Within this four months I have paid 80 guineas for one horse. He is completely lame and at Pinhel; 50 do. for another, left at Lamego, water in his chest. I have been forced to ride a black horse, which the General lent me, the whole campaign, as to buying horses at any price is impossible, except at Lisbon. Here I yesterday bought a mare blind of an eye, though a very nice one, for 40 gns. In this case, as you will suppose, with very expensive dress, I cannot save much towards my majority.

Since Rankin robbed me and was turned off, I have found it impossible to get a servant of any kind who would look after myself and horses, and am at last obliged to hire a Valet de Chambre (to avoid paying 800 Reis per diem to a Valet de place, who does nothing). He is highly recommended, has the care of everything, overlooks the stable, and finds himself in everything at 4 moidores a month. I shall not however keep him longer, when I can get an English groom.

I will send you the statement of losses at Coruña as soon as I can get an opportunity, and a printed form. The conduct of our Government towards the young men who entered the Portuguese service, and have exerted themselves very much, all meritorious young Officers, in not giving them the step of rank, in consequence of which most will quit it, at this most critical moment; and their giving rank to men totally out of the army, as Brigadiers, to come and command English Lt.-Cols. and Majors, is most extraordinary and disgusting. Beresford's exertions have been constant and unremitting and their excellent effect daily visible, but the Government have behaved shamefully to him in many respects...

I do not yet know when we quit Lisbon. It of course depends much on the movements of the enemy. You shall hear from me when we do. I believe our army is getting on very well, but, unless Government will make the Magistrates do their duty, and most severe examples of what deserters are caught, it (will be) impossible to keep them together, while they know that they can return home with impunity when they like. There is also a disgusting delay in getting anything done, when everything should be vigour and activity, and I really sometimes wonder at Beresford's perseverance and patience. A less firm man would have done nothing with them.

We look to Germany with the greatest anxiety. The renewal of hostilities is something, but the consequences are not less a matter of anxiety and fear than their Armistice. God prosper them. Their cause is that of Europe.

Adieu. Kindest love to all at home from, dearest friend, your ever affectionate Son."

The next letter, from Lieutenant-Colonel Frederick Ponsonby to his mother, Lady Bessborough, describes the days leading up to the battle of Salamanca in July 1812 and its aftermath. Ponsonby commanded Major-General Le Marchant's brigade the 12th Light Dragoons, and went on to fight at Waterloo, where he survived life-threatening injuries. The lead-up to Salamanca was quite extraordinary. For several days before the battle, French and British troops marched along either side of the Guarena River in sight of each other, but "perfectly quiet," as Ponsonby put it.

"Dearest M—we have had so much to do for the last end days that I scarcely know when I wrote last, but I shall begin from the 16th, when the enemy made a demonstration upon Toro, and Lord Wellington retreated. On the 18th the enemy crossed the Bridge of Tordesillas (Over the Douro River) in force, and drove in our pickets near La Nava which they occupied; on the morning of the 19th they advanced a strong body of Cavalry and Artillery on Castrejon, where we had two hours sharp canonading and skirmishing. I lost 16 men and 17 horses. About nine they moved some strong columns of infantry upon our left, and the two armies moved parallel to one another to the Height above Canizal, which the British occupied. A brigade of the enemy, having advanced too far on our left, was attacked and driven back with considerable loss.

The whole of the 19th, and till 4 the next day, the two armies remaining close to each other but perfectly quiet. At 4 in the afternoon of the 20th the enemy made a movement to our right; two brigades of Cavalry, and two of infantry made a corresponding movement, and we had a short cannonade, but did not suffer. On the morning of the 21st the whole of their Army was moving rapidly to our right, and we moved parallel to them all the way to Pitiagno. I had the rear guard, and very warm work for 15 hours. We lost a few men and horses by a cannonade, and skirmish, but we made a charge upon their tirailleurs, and knocked most of them over. On the 21st the enemy was seen to position over Huerta, and we retired to near Salamanca; in the evening we crossed the Tormes, in consequence of the enemy having made a movement to our right flank.

On the morning of the 22nd the enemy shewed a considerable force on our side of the river; a good deal of skirmishing and cannonading took place in which we did not suffer. Our baggage was ordered a good way to the rear, and preparations were making for our retreat, when Marmont, forgetting his former prudence and presuming upon the idea that Lord W. would not fight, made a movement to turn our right, and extended his left so much that an order was immediately given for attack. The lines were formed and moved on, and in spite of tremendous fire and other difficulties, they carried all before them. The heavy Drag's made a very successful charge, and the enemy's left was completely beat; it was getting very dark when Lord W. advanced the light divisions and first against their Right. I covered them with a squadron of the 12th and one of the 5th; we charged twice and in last went thro. two battalions of infantry. I was unfortunate enough to lose Dickens in this charge; he was leading a Squadron, and received a ball in his left breast. Just as we came up to the enemy's columns the officer who commanded the other squadron was also shot in the breast but not killed. Lord Wellington pushed on to Huerta the same night with two divisions and my detachments of cavalry.

On the morning of the 23rd we ascertained the direction of the flight of the enemy and pushed on them. The heavy German Brigade (KGL) and the rest of General Anson's coming up, Lord W. directed a Charge against the tail of the enemy's column which completely succeeded. The German's did wonders and an immense number of prisoners were taken. The same day we pursued them very close and attempted a charge upon their cavalry, but they were too strong for us. We did not however lose a man in the attempt. They have now got out of reach for the present but when the army is a little recovered from the fatigue, we shall push a little further.

I have knocked up all my horses; I lamed two on the day of the battle, broke my sword and lost my pistol. The weather has been uncommonly hot; we are always bivouacked; the fatigue, you may guess, has been great, provision not plenty and I never was better in my life."

Salamanca was among Wellington's most memorable battles, but Waterloo, one of the few battles to enter the language, is the one by which he is defined. As one of the most decisive battles in history, it ended a generation of fighting and ensured peace in Europe for 30 years. Contemporaries knew they were taking part in something momentous. A private in the Dragoons remarked that the Belgians were "sadly afeared of Boney's army," and Tsar Alexander of Russia, hearing the news of Bonaparte's escape, said to Wellington "It is for you to save the world again."

Right: The Scots Greys charge forward at the Battle of Waterloo.

Left: French Curassiers charge the Highlanders at the Battle of Waterloo.

Napoleon marched at the head of a 72,000-strong army. In this letter his secretary of the cabinet reports on conditions in the field to the Council of ministers in Paris.

"To Prince Joseph, President of the Council of Ministers, at Paris. Charleroi, June 15, 1815, nine o'clock in the evening.

My lord, it is nine o'clock in the evening, the Emperor, who has been on horseback since three o'clock in the morning, returned over-powered with fatigue. He has lain down on his bed to rest there a few hours. He must go back on horseback at midnight. His Majesty not being able to write to Your Highness charges me with the following:

The army has forced the Sambre close to Charleroi and pushed advanced guards half way to Charleroi at Namur and from Charleroi to Brussels. We took 1,500 prisoners and captured six pieces of artillery. Four Prussian regiments were crushed. The Emperor lost little. But he had a loss which is very-sensitive for him: it is his

Left: Napoleon retreats from Waterloo. He fled to Paris and abdicated on June 22, 1815, eventually surrendering to the British on July 15, 1815, at La Rochelle.

aide-de-camp, General Letort, who was killed on the Fleurus plateau leading a charge of cavalry. The enthusiasm of the inhabitants of Charleroi and all the countries which we cross cannot be described. This is the same feeling as in Burgundy.

The Emperor wishes, My Lord, that you share this news with the ministers, and that you see to the formalities for those who ask what to do.

It is possible that there will be a very-important affair tomorrow.

The first secretary of the cabinet,
Baron Fain"

Most of the surviving letters in this period are written by officers, and it is always refreshing to read the thoughts of an average soldier. This letter was written by Charles Stanley, a private in the King's Dragoon Guards a month before Waterloo. He seems quite impressed with Belgium and the inhabitants, and the English soldiers surmount the language problem by "makin moshins" (meaning "making motions," or "gesticulating"). Stanley is not altogether happy with his life and advises his friend not to join the army as it is a "Verry ruf Consarn" (meaning "a very rough concern," in other words, a tough life).

"Charles Stanley Privet Kings Dragun Guards To Mr. Cristerfer Alvey Booton Near Ollerton Nottinghamshire England

Wm. Fuller Lt.Col 1st. Dn. Gds. Brusels Flemish Flanders May 15th 1815

Dear Cusson I take this Oppetunety of Riting to you hoping this will find you all In gud helth as it leves me at Pressent I Thank God for It I have ad a Verry Ruf march Since i sow you at Booton we am onley 15 miles From Mr. Boney Part Harmey wish we Expect To have a Rap at him Exerry Day We have the Most Cavilrey of the English that Ever was None at One time and in Gud Condishon and Gud sperrits we have lost a few horses by hour Marshing I have the Plesure to say my horse Is Better Everry Day Wish i think im to be the Best frend i have at Pressant there is no dout Of us Beting the Confounded Rascald it ma Cost Me my Life and a meaney more that will onley Be the forting of War my Life i set ne store By at all this is the finest Cuntrey Exer i So far before England the peepal is so Sivel thare land Coltevated so well most of them as a littel land and they Havit as Clen as a Jentelmas Garden tha are Sadley a frad of Boneys Harmey Comming a gane he Distrest them so before we have sum Littel trubel to make them Understand us not noing thare Languige we do a grate del By makin moshins

We have one gud thing Cheap that is Tobaco and Everrything a-Cordnley Tobaco is 4d Per 1b Gin is 1s 8d Per Galland that is 2 $\frac{1}{2}$ Per Quart and Everrything In Perposion hour alounse Per Day is One Pound of Beef a Pound and half of Bred half a Pint o Gin But the worst of all we dont get it Regeler and If we dont get it the Day it is due we Luse it wish It is ofton the Case i asure you My Dear Lad I hop Wot Ever may Comacros your mind to trobel You wish i hope nothing will I hope you never will think Of Being a Soldier I Asure you it is a Verry Ruf Consarn I have Rote to my Sister Ann and I ham afraid She thinks the trubel to mush to answer my Letter wen Over at Woodhous she semed Verry Desires of mi Ritting to her out of site ou of mind I have not ad the Pleasure of Ling in a Bed sinco In the Cuntrey thank God the Weather is fine Wish is in hour faver we Get no Pay at all onley hour Bed and mete and Gin we have 10d Per Day soped from us wish we shal Reseive wen six months is Expiered I thank God i have a frend with me wish i Find verry yous fol to me i asure you (I have not any Time to say any) I hope you will Excuse my Bad Inditing and Spelling my Love to Aunt and Cus-sons Mrs Darby Cusson Joseph and family at Edwinsto and all that Thinks well to ask after me my Duty to Mother wen you see her.

If you think well to answer my Letter wish I should Be Verry gad You would I Should be Verry Glad To here from you all Plese to Derect to me

To Charles Stanley the fost or Kings Dragun Gurds Kings Troop Brstels, Flanders or Elswere

Hour Rigment is Brgaded with the Two Rigments of Life Guards and the Oxferd Bluse So no more at Prssant from your Ever wel wisher C. Stanly God Bles you all

Be so gud as to Pay a Penny with your Letter and see it marked Post Pade"

[Transcript:

Dear Cousin, I take this opportunity of writing to you hoping this will find all in good health as it leaves me at present. I thank God for it as I have had a very rough march since I saw you at Booton. We are only 15 miles from Mr Bonaparte's army which we expect to have a rap at every day. We have the most cavalry of the English that ever was…and in good condition and good spirits. We have a lost a few horses by our marching. I have the pleasure to say my horse is better every day, which I think him to be the best friend I have at present. There is no doubt of us beating the confounded rascal [although] it may cost me my life and a meaney more that will only be the for-tunes of war. My life I set no store by at all. This is the finest country ever so far. Before England, the people are so civil, their land is culti-vated so well; most of them have a little land and they have it as clean as a gentleman's garden. They are sadly afraid of Boney's army com-ing again— he distressed them so before. We have some little trouble to make them understand us, not knowing their language. We do a great deal by making motions.

We have one good thing cheap—that is tobacco and everything accordingly. Tobacco is 4d per pound; gin is 1s 8d per gallon (that is 2$\frac{1}{2}$ per quart), and everything is in proportion. Our allowance per day is one pound of beef, a pound and a half of bread, half a pint of gin. But worst of all, we don't get it regular, and if we don't get it the day, we lose it, which is often the case.

I assure you my dear lad I hope what ever may come across your mind to trouble you will never think of being a soldier. I assure you it is a very rough concern. I have written to my sister Ann and I am afraid she thinks it too much trouble to answer my letter, when over at Woodhouse she seemed very desirous of my writing to her. Out of sight, out of mind.

I have not had the pleasure of lying in a bed since. In the country thank God the weather is fine, which is in our favor. We get no pay at all, only our bed and meat and gin. We have 10d per day stopped from us and which we shall receive when six months has expired. I thank God I have a friend with me which I find very useful to me, I assure you (I have no time to mention them). I hope you will excuse my bad writing and spelling. My love to Aunt and cousins Mrs Darby, cousin Joseph, and the family at Edwinstowe and all that thinks well to ask after me. My duty to mother when you see her.

If you think well to answer my letter, I shall be very glad to hear from you all. Please to direct it to me, Charles Stanley, the First or King's Dragoon Guards, King's troop, Brussels, Flanders or elsewhere.

Our regiment is brigaded with the two regiments of Life Guards and the Oxford Blues. So no more at present from your ever well-wisher C Stanley. God Bless you all

Be so good as to pay a penny with your letter and see it marked post paid.]

This amazingly vivid account of a skirmish during the battle of Waterloo was written by Rifleman John Lewis of the 95th Rifles shortly after the battle. He describes how he dodged death as the men around him were felled by French bullets, although he suffered what all riflemen dreaded, a bent barrel, making his rifle useless.

"My front rank man was wounded by part of a shell through his foot, and he dropt as we were advancing; I covered the next man I saw, and had not walked twenty steps before a musket-shot came sideways and took his nose clean off; and then I covered another man. Just after that the man stood next to me on my left had his right arm shot off by a 9-pound shot just above the elbow, and he turned and caught hold of me with his left hand, and the blood run all over my trousers; we were advancing and he dropt directly.

Boney's cuirassiers, all dressed in armour, made a charge at us; we saw them coming, and we closed in and formed a square just as

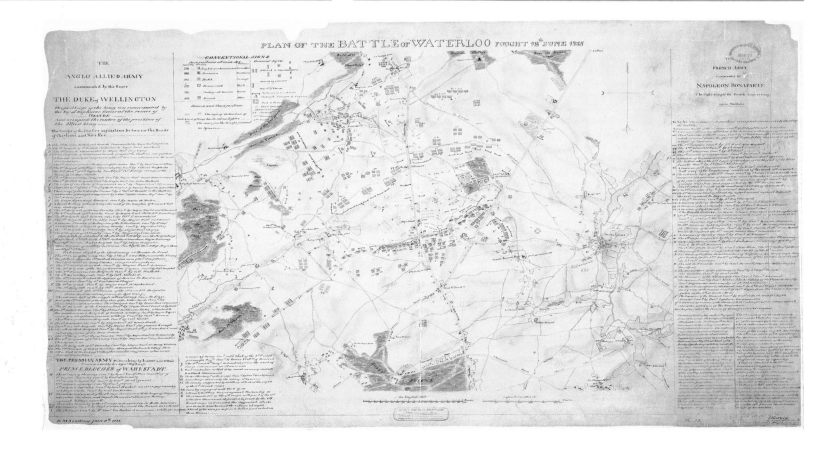

Right: A plan of the Battle of Waterloo June 18, 1815.

they came within ten yards of us... As I was loading my rifle, one of their shots came and struck it, not two inches above my right hand, as I was ramming down the ball, and bent the barrel so I could not get the ball down. A nine-pounder shot came and cut the serjeant of our company in two; he was not above three file from me. So I threw down my rifle and took his, as it was not hurt at the time... Seeing we had lost so many men and all our commanding officers, my heart began to fail but, while we was in square, the Duke of Wellington and his staff came up to us in all the fire and saw we had lost all our commanding officers, he himself gave the words of command— '95th, unfix your swords, left face and extend yourselves once more. We shall soon have them over the hill.' Then he rode away to our right, and how he escaped being shot God only knows, for all that time shot was flying like hail stones."

For Wellington, acknowledged as the hero of the hour, the day after the battle seems to have been taken up with administration, as he penned letters to the allied governments reporting his victory, and also found time to write letters of condolence to the families of some of the officers lost in the battle. His "Waterloo despatch," initially addressed to Lord Bathhurst, the Minister for War, was printed in full in *The Times* four days after the battle and has been criticized for failing to acknowledge the contribution of many units and individuals. In fact, it is a document written in Wellington's characteristically economic and terse style which conveys an account of exactly what happened with little elaboration.

"June 19th, 1815
To Earl Bathurst. 'Waterloo, 19th June' 1815.

My Lord
Buonaparte, having collected the 1st, 2nd, 3rd, 4th, and 6th corps of the French army, and the Imperial Guards, and nearly all the cavalry, on the Sambre, and between that river and the Meuse, between the 10th and 14th of the month, advanced on the 15th and attacked the Prussian posts at Thuin and Lobbes, on the Sambre, at day-light in the morning.

Above: Portrait of the Duke of Wellington. Wellington later referred to Waterloo as "a battle of giants."

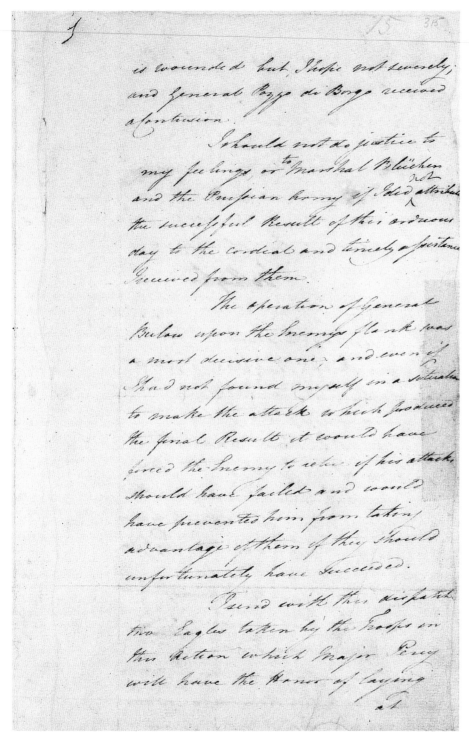

Above: The original despatch from Wellington to Earl Bathurst, the Minister for War, giving an account of the Battle of Waterloo.

I did not hear of these events till in the evening of the 15th; and I immediately ordered the troops to prepare to march, and, afterwards to march to their left, as soon as I had intelligence from other quarters to prove that the enemy's movement upon Charleroi was the real attack.

The enemy drove the Prussian posts from the Sambre on that day; and General Ziethen, who commanded the corps which had been at Charleroi, retired upon Fleurus; and Marshal Prince Blücher concentrated the Prussian army upon Sombref, holding the villages in front of his position of St. Amand and Ligny.

The enemy continued his march along the road from Charleroi towards Bruxelles; and, on the same evening, the 15th, attacked a brigade of the army of the Netherlands, under the Prince de Weimar, posted at Frasne, and forced it back to the farm house, on the same road, called Les Quatre Bras.

The Prince of Orange immediately reinforced this brigade with another of the same division, under General Perponcher, and, in the morning early, regained part of the ground which had been lost, so as to have the command of the communication leading from Nivelles and Bruxelles with Marshal Blücher's position.

In the mean time, I had directed the whole army to march upon Les Quatre Bras; and the 5th division, under Lieut. General Sir Thomas Picton, arrived at about half past two in the day, followed by the corps of troops under the Duke of Brunswick, and afterwards by the contingent of Nassau.

At this time the enemy commenced an attack upon Prince Blücher with his whole force, excepting the 1st and 2nd corps, and a corps of cavalry under General Kellermann, with which he attacked our post at Les Quatre Bras.

The Prussian army maintained their position with their usual gallantry and perseverance against a great disparity of numbers, as the 4th corps of their army, under General Bülow, had not joined; and I was not able to assist them as I wished, as I was attacked myself, and the troops, the cavalry in particular, which had a long distance to march, had not arrived.

We maintained our position also, and completely defeated and repulsed all the enemy's attempts to get possession of it. The enemy repeatedly attacked us with a large body of infantry and cavalry, supported by a numerous and powerful artillery. He made several charges with the cavalry upon our infantry, but all were repulsed in the steadiest manner.

In this affair, His Royal Highness the Prince of Orange, the Duke of Brunswick, and Lieut. General Sir Thomas Picton, and Major Generals Sir James Kempt and Sir Denis Pack, who were engaged from the commencement of the enemy's attack, highly distinguished themselves, as well as Lieut. General Charles Baron Alten, Major General Sir C. Halkett, Lieut. General Cooke, and Major Generals Maitland and Byng, as they successively arrived. The troops of the 5th division, and those of the Brunswick corps, were long and severely engaged, and conducted themselves with the utmost gallantry. I must particularly mention the 28th, 42nd, 79th, and 92nd regiments, and the battalion of Hanoverians.

Our loss was great, as your Lordship will perceive by the enclosed return; and I have particularly to regret His Serene Highness the Duke of Brunswick, who fell fighting gallantly at the head of his troops.

Although Marshal Blücher had maintained his position at Sombref, he still found himself much weakened by the severity of the contest in which he had been engaged, and, as the 4th corps had not arrived, he determined to fall back and to concentrate his army upon Wavre; and he marched ill the night, after the action was over.

This movement of the Marshal rendered necessary a corresponding one upon my part; and I retired from the farm of Quatre Bras upon Genappe, and thence upon Waterloo, the next morning, the 17th, at ten o'clock.

The enemy made no effort to pursue Marshal Blücher. On the contrary, a patrole which I sent to Sombref in the morning found all quiet; and the enemy's vedettes fell back as the patrole advanced. Neither did he attempt to molest our march to the rear, although made in the middle of the day, excepting by following, with a large body of cavalry brought from his right, the cavalry under the Earl of Uxbridge.

(Lieut. Colonel the Hon. Alexander Gordon was sent, escorted by a squadron of the 10th hussars, to communicate with the Prussian head quarters, as to cooperation with the British army ordered to retire to the position in front of Waterloo.)

This gave Lord Uxbridge an opportunity of charging—them with the 1st Life Guards, upon their débouché from the village of Genappe, upon which occasion his Lordship has declared himself to be well satisfied with that regiment.

The position which I took up in front of Waterloo crossed the high roads from Charleroi and Nivelles, and had its right thrown back to a ravine near Merke Braine, which was occupied, and its left extended to a height above the hamlet Ter la Haye, which was likewise occupied. In front of the right centre, and near the Nivelles road, we occupied the house and gardens of Hougoumont, which covered the return of that flank; and in front of the left centre we occupied the farm of La Haye Sainte. By our left we communicated with Marshal Prince Blücher at Wavre, through Ohain; and the Marshal had promised me that, in case we should be attacked, he would support me with one or more corps, as might be necessary.

The enemy collected his army, with the exception of the 3rd corps, which had been sent to observe Marshal Blücher, on a range of heights in our front, in the course of the night of the 17th and yesterday morning, and at about ten o'clock he commenced a furious attack upon our post at Hougoumont. I had occupied that post with a detachment from General Byng's brigade of Guards, which was in position in its rear; and it was for some time under the command of Lieut. Colonel Macdonell, and afterwards of Colonel Home; and I am happy to add that it was maintained throughout the day with the utmost gallantry by these brave troops, notwithstanding the repeated efforts of large bodies of the enemy to obtain possession of it.

This attack upon the right of our centre was accompanied by a very heavy cannonade upon our whole line, which was destined to support the repeated attacks of cavalry and infantry, occasionally mixed, but sometimes separate, which were made upon it. In one of these the enemy carried the farm house of La Haye Sainte, as the detachment of the light battalion of the German Legion, which occupied it, had expended all its ammunition; and the enemy occupied the only communication there was with them.

The enemy repeatedly charged our infantry with his cavalry, but these attacks were uniformly unsuccessful; and they afforded opportunities to our cavalry to charge, in one of which Lord E. Somerset's brigade, consisting of the Life Guards, the Royal Horse Guards, and 1st dragoon guards, highly distinguished themselves, as did that of Major General Sir William Ponsonby, having taken many prisoners and an eagle.

These attacks were repeated till about seven in the evening, when the enemy made a desperate effort with cavalry and infantry, supported by the fire of artillery, to force our left centre, near the farm of La Haye Sainte, which, after a severe contest, was defeated; and, having observed that the troops retired from this attack in great confusion, and that the march of General Bülow's corps, by Frischermont, upon Planchenois and La Belle Alliance, had begun to take effect, and as I could perceive the fire of his cannon, and as Marshal Prince Blücher had joined in person with a corps of his army to the left of our line by Ohain, I determined to attack the enemy, and immediately advanced the whole line of infantry, supported by the cavalry and artillery. The attack succeeded in every point: the enemy was forced from his positions on the heights, and fled in the utmost confusion, leaving behind him, as far as I could judge, 150 pieces of cannon, with their ammunition, which fell into our hands.

I continued the pursuit till long after dark, and then discontinued it only on account of the fatigue of our troops, who had been engaged during twelve hours, and because I found myself on the same road with Marshal Blücher, who assured me of his intention to follow the enemy throughout the night. He has sent me word this morning that he had taken 60 pieces of cannon belonging to the Imperial Guard, and several carriages, baggage, &c., belonging to Buonaparte, in Genappe.

I propose to move this morning upon Nivelles, and not to discontinue my operations.

Your Lordship will observe that such a desperate action could not be fought, and such advantages could not be gained, without great loss; and I am sorry to add that ours has been immense. In Lieut. General Sir Thomas Picton His Majesty has sustained the loss of an officer who has frequently distinguished himself in his service, and he fell gloriously leading his division to a charge with bayonets, by which one of the most serious attacks made by the enemy on our position was repulsed, The Earl of Uxbridge, after having successfully got through this arduous day, received a wound by almost the last shot fired, which will, I am afraid, deprive His Majesty for some time of his services

His Royal Highness the Prince of Orange distinguished himself by his gallantry and conduct, till he received a wound from a musket ball through the shoulder, which obliged him to quit the field.

It gives me the greatest satisfaction to assure your Lordship that the army never, upon any occasion, conducted itself better. The division of Guards, under Lieut. General Cooke, who is severely wounded, Major General Maitland, and Major General Byng, set an example which was followed by all; and there is no officer nor description of troops that did not behave well.

I must, however, particularly mention, for His Royal Highness's approbation, Lieut. General Sir H. Clinton, Major General Adam, Lieut. General Charles Baron Alten (severely wounded), Major General Sir Colin Halkett (severely wounded), Colonel Ompteda, Colonel Mitchell (commanding a brigade of the 4th division), Major Generals Sir James Kempt and Sir D. Pack, Major General Lambert, Major General Lord E. Somerset, Major General Sir W. Ponsonby, Major General Sir C. Grant, and Major General Sir H. Vivian, Major General Sir O. Vandeleur, and Major General Count Dornberg.

I am also particularly indebted to General Lord Hill for his assistance and conduct upon this, as upon all former occasions.

The artillery and engineer departments were conducted much to my satisfaction by Colonel Sir George Wood and Colonel Smyth; and I had every reason to be satisfied with the conduct of the Adjutant General, Major General Barnes, who was wounded, and of the Quarter Master General, Colonel De Lancey, who was killed by a cannon shot in the middle of the action. This officer is a serious loss to His Majesty's service, and to me at this moment.

I was likewise much indebted to the assistance of Lieut. Colonel Lord FitzRoy Somerset, who was severely wounded, and of the officers composing my personal Staff, who have suffered severely in this action. Lieut. Colonel the Hon. Sir Alexander Gordon, who has died of his wounds, was a most promising officer, and is a serious loss to His Majesty's service.

General Kruse, of the Nassau service, likewise conducted himself much to my satisfaction; as did General Tripp, commending the heavy brigade of cavalry, and General Vanhope, commanding a Brigade of infantry in the service of the King, of the Netherlands.

General Pozzo di Borgo, General Baron Vincent, General Muffling, and General Alava, were in the field during the action, and rendered me every assistance in their power. Baron Vincent is wounded, but I hope not severely; and General Pozzo di Borgo received a contusion.

I should not do justice to my own feelings, or to Marshal Blücher and the Prussian army, if I did not attribute the successful result of this arduous day to the cordial and timely assistance I received from them. The operation of General Bülow upon the enemy's flank was a most decisive one; and, even if I had not found myself in a situation to make the attack which produced the final result, it would have forced the enemy to retire if his attacks should have failed, and would have prevented him from taking advantage of them if they should unfortunately have succeeded.

Since writing the above, I have received a report that Major General Sir William Ponsonby is killed; and, in announcing this intelligence to your Lordship, I have to add the expression of my grief for the fate of an officer who had already rendered very brilliant and important services, and was an ornament to his profession.

I send with this dispatch three eagles, taken by the troops in this action, which Major Percy will have the honor of laying at the feet of His Royal Highness. I beg leave to recommend him to your Lordship's protection.

I have the honor to be, &c. WELLINGTON."

Wellington went on to list the numbers of dead and wounded. Waterloo may have been a glorious victory, but he could not forget the losses: some 15,000 allied troops were killed or wounded, and 25,000 French. He is quoted as saying "Well thank God I don't know what it is to lose a battle; but certainly nothing can be more painful than to gain one with the loss of so many of one's friends." This letter to the Earl of Aberdeen reports the death of his brother, Wellington's trusted ADC, Sir Alexander Gordon.

"To the Earl of Aberdeen, K.T.
'Bruxelles, 19th June, 1815.

My Dear Lord,

You will readily give credit to the existence of the extreme grief with which I announce to you the death of your gallant brother, in consequence of a wound received in our great battle of yesterday.

He had served me most zealously and usefully for many years, and on many trying occasions; but he had never rendered himself more useful, and had never distinguished himself more, than in our late actions.

He received the wound which occasioned his death when rallying one of the Brunswick battalions which was shaking a little; and he lived long enough to be informed by myself of the glorious result of our actions, to which he had so much contributed by his active and zealous assistance.

I cannot express to you the regret and sorrow with which I look round me, and contemplate the loss which I have sustained, particularly in your brother. The glory resulting from such actions, so dearly bought, is no consolation to me, and I cannot suggest it as any to you and his friends; but I hope that it may be expected that this last one has been so decisive, as that no doubt remains that our exertions and our individual losses will be rewarded by the early attainment of our just object. It is then that the glory of the actions in which our friends and relations have fallen will be some consolation for their loss.

Believe me &c. WELLINGTON

Your brother had a black horse, given to him, I believe, by Lord Ashburnham, which I will keep till I hear from you what you wish should be done with it."

Wellington apparently wept over the losses of Waterloo, but in public remained the image of the "Iron Duke;" he revealed his real feelings in a letter to his brother William: "it was the most desperate business I ever was in. I never took so much trouble about any Battle & never was so near being beat. Our loss is immense particularly in that best of all Instruments, British infantry. I never saw the infantry behave so well."[1]

[1]Quoted in *Wellington, The Years of the Sword* by Elizabeth Longford.

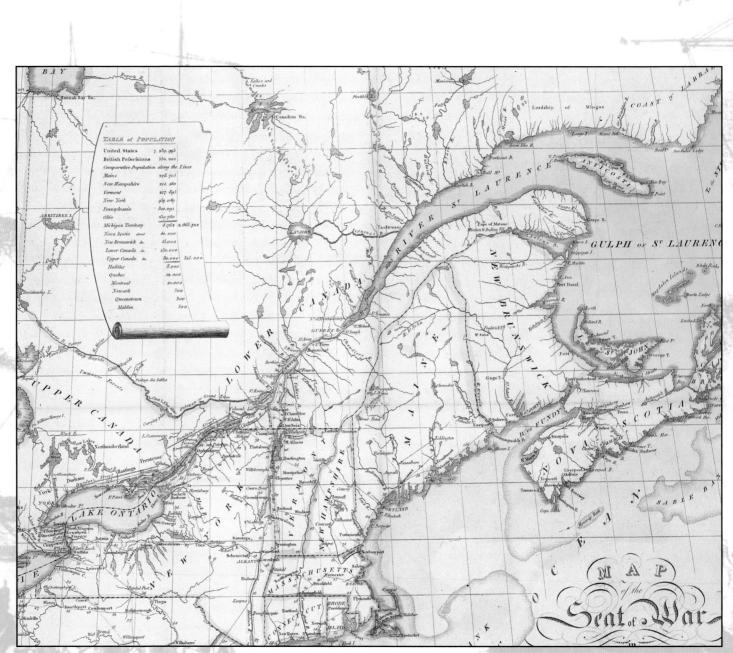

Right: Published by John Melish of Philadelphia in March 1813, this map shows the constituent states and territories of America along with the adjoining British territories at the time of the War of 1812.

Far right: Major General Andrew Jackson (later 7th president of the USA) was one of America's most competent generals and won a stunning victory over the British at New Orleans in 1815.

The War of 1812

The War of 1812 was a curious war for the British, and was almost a sideshow to the more immediate threats posed by the Napoleonic Wars in Europe. For the new American nation, however, it was the first test of their strength and unity in the face of foreign oppression. In one of his letters, Ensign Thomas Warner asked to be remembered to "old seventisixer," presumably a friend or relative who was a veteran of the action in 1776 during the American War of Independence. Warner's identification with him and his cause is indicative of the reason why the war of 1812 is often considered to be America's second war of independence.

Despite losing the 13 colonies in 1783, Britain retained a profitable colonial foothold in Canada and the natural resources of that country (in particular timber for ships) became especially vital to the British once access to the Baltic ports was denied by the French. The British attempted to ban all trade with France, even on the part of neutral countries, as part of their war with Napoleon. Many American merchant ships had been seized as part of this policy. The British also demanded the right to board American merchant ships, allegedly in search of British nationals, with the aim of impressing them for service in the Royal Navy. This heavy handed method of recruitment often extended to unwilling U.S. nationals and was both unpopular in purely practical terms and damaging to the pride of a relatively new nation. The British tried to extend these practices to U.S. warships, provoking a series of inflammatory naval incidents. Diplomatic efforts proved too slow to be effective. On June 16, 1812, the British government stepped back, announcing that it would end these practices, but news took at least a month to reach America from Britain, and on June 18, 1812, President James Madison signed a declaration of war, "for Free Trade and Sailors' rights."

The American nation was ill-prepared for war, but fired by patriotic fervor began a three-pronged offensive against Canada. By mid-October the westernmost attacks had failed, and Forts Mackinac and Dearborn were surrendered to the British along with Detroit. The Americans also launched

Right: The death of the British commander Sir Edward Packenham at the Battle of New Orleans, 1815. Two thousand British troops died during this ill-advised attack, an endeavor criticized by Packenham's brother-in-law, Wellington.

Left: Jackson commanded a motley army of some 5,000 troops drawn from militia, slaves, freebooters, and civilian volunteers. However, they formed a cohesive defensive force which mowed down the assaulting British troops at New Orleans.

an attack across the Niagara frontier, which foundered in October 1812 when nearly 1,000 U.S. troops were surrounded at Queenston, Canada.

The naval war, however, was initially an outstanding success for the United States, who won a series of single-ship engagements with British frigates. In his letter, Thomas Warner was rightly proud of "the beauty of our little fleet" that he believed could "flog twice their number without any difficulty." They imposed the worst defeats on the Royal Navy for a generation but, their success was short-lived and in December 1812, Britain imposed a crippling blockade on the northeast seaboard, virtually imprisoning U.S. warships (all 16 of them) in their ports.

During 1813, the Americans made further attempts to invade Canada, generally without success, although they forced the British to retreat eastward from the Detroit region. American land forces needed the support of the navy in order to sustain a victory and they won back Detroit largely because of Perry's naval victory on Lake Erie. By 1814, Britain could afford to concentrate larger numbers of troops on the American war, as Napoleon's exile made an uneasy peace in Europe. At the same time, the United States

verged on bankruptcy after two years of punitive commercial blockades and many Americans wanted peace. In the summer of 1814, the British marched into Washington and burned down the White House, while a further 10,000 veteran troops invaded from Montreal. The Americans seemed doomed, but on September 11, 1814, Captain Thomas Macdonough destroyed the British fleet at Plattsburg Bay (Lake Champlain), and the British, fearing a severed line of communication, retreated.

This defeat prompted British peace negotiators to forgo all territorial demands, although they did not stretch to recognizing America's rights as a neutral nation. The Americans were happy to end the war without any territorial losses and ratified the Treaty of Ghent on December 24, 1814. News continued to travel slowly, however, and in January 1815 the British launched an ill-advised attack on New Orleans and were savagely beaten back by General Andrew Jackson. British casualties amounted to 2,000, whereas America suffered a loss of 100. News of this victory emerged at the same time as news of the peace, and it seemed to many Americans that the war had ended in triumph.

Although poorly prepared for war, the United States army began on the offensive in 1812, sending regular troops and hurriedly recruited volunteers north to attack Canada. Baltimore silversmith Thomas Warner joined Captain Stephen Moore's company of U.S. Volunteers as a junior officer and served for a year. Five of his letters home survive and it is interesting to note how his mood changes subtly as the campaign progresses. His first letter is full of jingoistic patriotism, the second proud of his unit's exploits, and the later ones of a more somber mood as he and his comrades suffer at the hands of the British. Ensign Warner marched from Baltimore to camp at Sackett's Harbor and fought at the battle of York (now Toronto) under the colorful General Zebulon Pike, who was killed during the engagement.

"Carlile October 7 1812

Dear Mary

We arrived here after fatiguing a march to some of our men on Saturday evening, very good weather until the last day when it rained the whole day. The water ran down the mountains in torrents, however our men were in the highest spirits singing and joking each other all the way. Will have not a man on the sick list. For my own part I never was healthier in my life. In high spirits.

The citizens of Carlile have treated us with the greatest hospitality. They would not suffer us to pitch our tents until Sunday. They came forward and offered their houses beds and provisions for our accommodation gratis. On yesterday they presented the whole corps with an ellegant dinner and plenty of wine to drink their healths with which was done with enthusiasm. In truth their hospitality is beyond anything I ever experienced. Please to inform Mr. Barckley I saw his Brother Robert who was well. I met here a great number of old acquaintances Brother officers who treated me with the most marked attention. Should you be acquainted with any of those particular Ladies of the seventh ward who presented us our stand of colours you will please inform them they were so much admired we were obliged to display them.

My dear wife you will please inform my mother, my brothers and sisters and my friends also of my health etc. tell them I would write them but the extreem difficulty an officer is under of getting paper, time and other necessarys totally incapassitate me. Therefore they must wait with patience.

Do be pleased to write me how my dear children are and yourself as you and them are the only thing that prey on my mind I hope you will excuse me for not calling to bid you adieu as the trial would have been too great for me to bear At the same time remember you are a soldiers wife—and one who loves you dearly give them one kiss and tell them their father puts up a prayer to heaven for their welfare.

Mr. Nolan, Our waggoner will be in town on Saturday and if you or any of my friends will write he will bring them direct to me. He will be found at Mr. Leypolds. Afterwards the letters must be directed to Niagara. Be pleased to tell Mr. Barckley to give my respects to Mr. Richardson, Mr. Sollers, Haslet, Taylor, Barry, Myers & all enquiring friends

—particularly request Mr. Barckley to write by Nolan, give my sincere love and respects to Groff and my Brother Andrew—except for yourself and Children my love and esteem

Mrs. Mary Ann Warner

Your affectionate husband until death
Thomas Warner"

Six weeks later, Warner was at Buffalo, dramatically writing that they were about "to embark for Canada—consequently it will be liberty or death." By April 1813, Warner and his men were still preparing for action but were proud of themselves and their reputation.

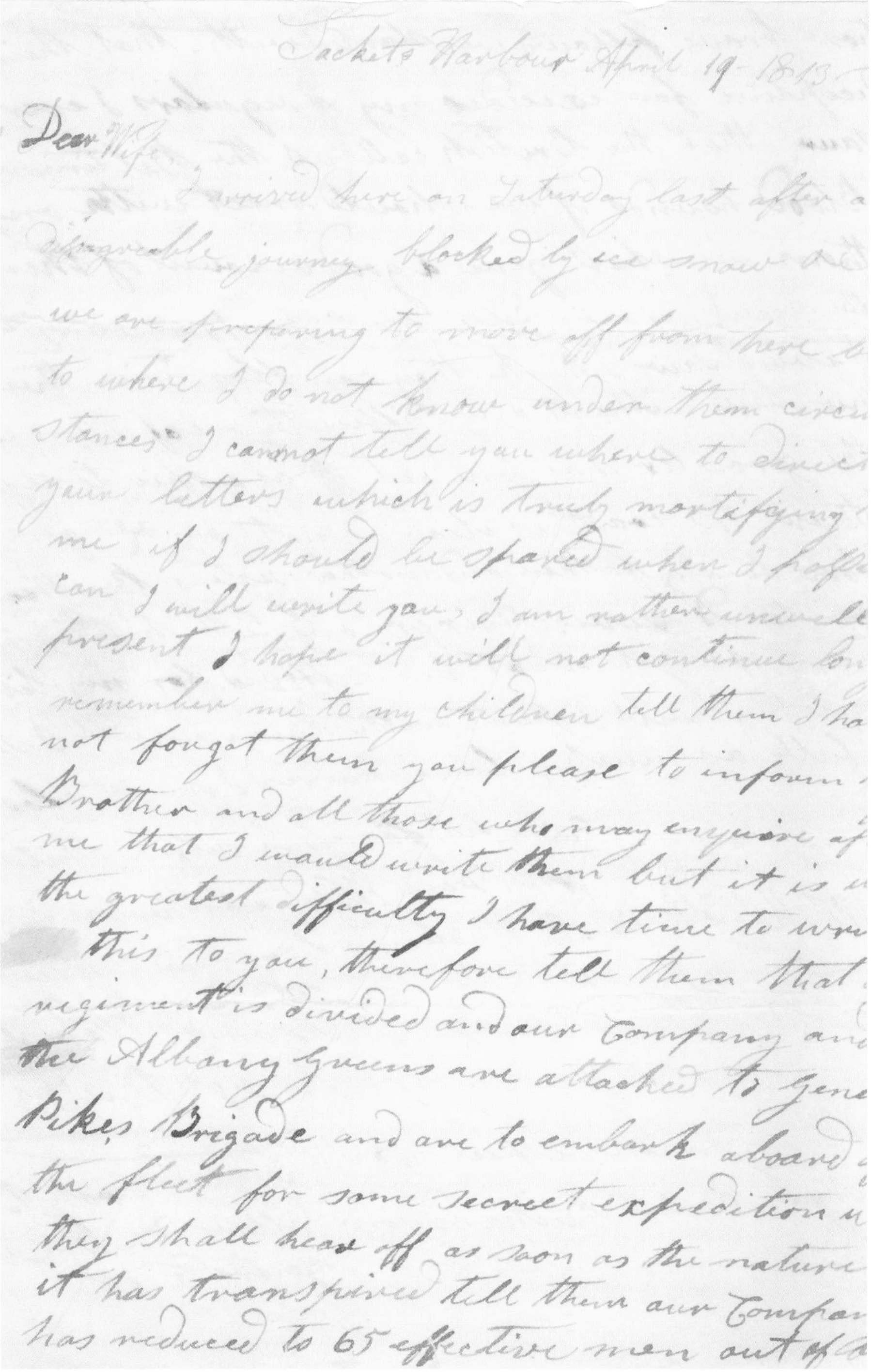

"Sackets Harbour April 19 1813

My Dear Wife,

I arrived here on Saturday last after a disagreeable journey blocked by ice, snow, etc. We are preparing to move off from here but to where I do not know. Under the circumstances I cannot tell you where to direct your letters which is truly mortifying to me. If I should be spared when I possibly can I will write you.

I am rather unwell at present. I hope it will not continue long. Remember me to my children. Tell them I have not forgot them. You please inform my Brother and all those who may enquire after me that I would write them but it is with the greatest difficulty I have time to write this to you, therefore tell them that our regiment is divided and our Company and the Albany Greens are attached to general Pikes Brigade and are to embark abroad of the fleet for some

Far left, above, and following pages: The original copy of letters written by Thomas Warner, who joined Captain Stephen Moore's company of U.S. volunteers as a junior officer, serving for a year.

secret expedition which they shall hear of as soon as the nature of it has transpired.

Tell them our Company has reduced to 65 effective men out of all those brave fellow we started with. That their discipline far exceeded any regulars I ever saw, that the British call us the Baltimore Blood hounds. If we should meet with any of them we shall give a good account of them.

The beauty of our little fleet surpasses anything I ever saw, I think they can flog twice their number without any difficulty. One of them, called the growler, has gone out as a spie to see whether the coast is clear or not etc. etc.

Give my love to my father and mother sisters, brothers & to old seventisixer and tell him I have not forgot what he suffered for my liberties. Neither will I part with them until I suffer full as much. Being hurried I must close.

Except for yourself and children My Dear Wife a father and Husband's love and esteem

Thomas Warner Ensign"

Ten days later, Warner had experienced his first battle and his letter with its repeated references to his children, reflects the sheer joy and sense of surprise that he has survived at all.

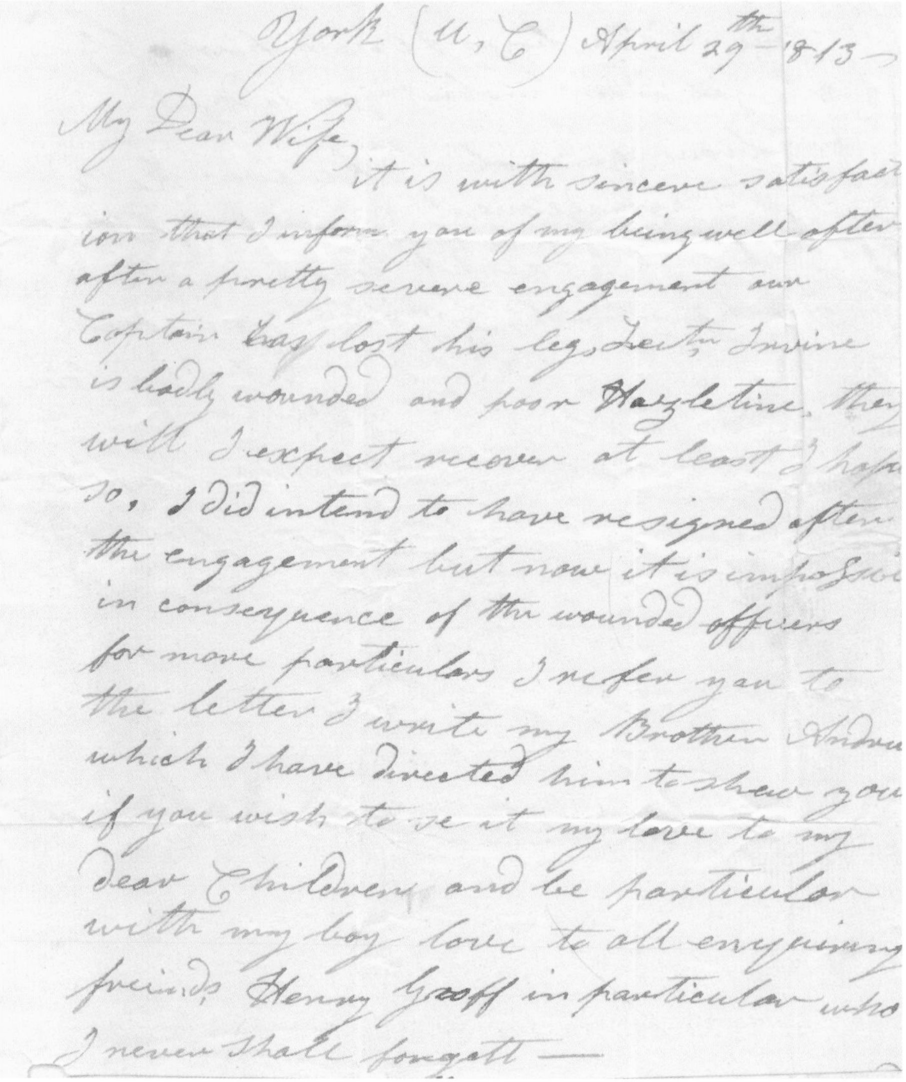

"York (U.C) April 29th—1813

My Dear Wife,

It is with sincere satisfaction that I inform you of my being well after a pretty severe engagement. Our Captain has lost his leg, Lester Irvine is badly wounded and poor Hazeltine. They will I expect recover, at least I hope so.

I did intend to have resigned after the engagement but now it is impossible in consequence of the wounded officers. For more particulars I refer you to the letter I write my Brother Andrew which I have directed him to show you if you wish to see it.

My love to my dear children and be particular with my boy. Love to all enquiring friends, Henry Groff in particular who I shall never forgett.

My love to the boys. I shall probably write you again in about 8 or 10 days. Our brave general Pike was killed in the engagement.

Except for yourself and Children my sincere love and esteem—

Thomas Warner
Ensign Balt. Volt."

York (U, C) April 29th 1813

My Dear Wife,
It is with sincere satisfaction that I inform you of my being well after after a pretty severe engagement our Captain has lost his leg, Lieut. Irvine is badly wounded and poor Hazletine, they will I expect recover at least I hope so, I did intend to have resigned after the engagement but now it is impossible in consequence of the wounded offiers for more particulars I refer you to the letter I write my Brother Andrew which I have directed him to shew you if you wish to se it my love to my dear Children and be particular with my boy love to all enquiring freinds Henry Groff in particular who I never shall forgett —

By now, Warner wants to go home—miserable and ill, he mourns the loss of both his friends and his possessions. And the vagaries of the field postal service seem to irk him. He was honorably discharged from the army in September 1813.

"Camp near 4 Mile Creek (at Niagara) May 10, 1813

My Dear Wife,

I wrote you one letter dated at Sackets Harbour and one dated at Little York upper Canada in which I directed you not to write me and one I wrote my Brother Andrew directed him the same. 2 of these letters were wrote after the engagement.

I gave my brother as accurate account of the Engagement as I could. You will please tell him that it is my request he should send brother William a copy of it at my request.

Poor Hazletine died of his wounds 9 or 10 days after the Engagement. As we have all returned to the American shore again and expect to remain here 3 or 4 weeks, you will please direct your letters to Niagara and inform those who will please write me to direct them in the same manner.

I am very unwell today with the dysentery but hope it will not last long.

My love to my Children and all my friends. Except for yourself and Children my Dear Wife my best love and esteem

Thomas Warner
Ens. B. Volt.

N.B. I left my trunk watch and clothes at Sackets Harbour in care of Wm. Olcott—pursers Steward on board the Hammilton. God knows whether I shall ever get it or not.

Yours, T. W."

Captain Isaac Chauncey's letter to the U.S. Secretary of the Navy about the capture of York reports on the very battle that Ensign Warner fought in. U.S. strategy was simple: they intended to mass a force at Sackett's Harbor

during the winter of 1812 and then ferry troops across Lake Ontario to the lightly defended Kingston as soon as the spring thaw permitted. The British learned of these plans and sent troops across the unforgiving winter countryside to reinforce Kingston. The Americans still possessed the superior force, but they feared defeat and decided to attack York instead, which was the Upper Canadian capital and far less important strategically.

"U.S.S. Madison, at anchor off York, Upper Canada, 28 April 1813

Agreeably to your instructions and arrangements with Major General Dearborn, I took on board the squadron under my command, the general and suite, and about 1700 troops, and left Sackett's Harbor on the 25th instant for this place. We arrived here yesterday morning, and took a position about one mile south and westward of the enemy's principal fort, and as near the shore as we could, with safety to the vessels. The place fixed upon by the major general and myself for landing the troops, was the site of the old French fort Tarento.

The debarkation commenced about 8 o'clock A.M. and was completed about ten. The wind blowing heavy from the eastward, the boats fell to leeward of the position fixed upon, and were, in consequence, exposed to a galling fire of the enemy, who had taken a position in a thick wood near where the first troops landed; however, the cool intrepidity of the officers and men overcame every obstacle.

Their attack upon the enemy was so vigorous, that he fled in every direction, leaving a great many of his killed and wounded upon the field. As soon as the troops were landed, I directed the schooners to take a position near the forts, in order that the attack on them by the army and navy might be simultaneous. The schooners were obliged to beat up to their position, which they did in a very handsome order, under a very heavy fire from the enemy's batteries, and took a position within about six hundred yards of their principal fort, and opened a heavy cannonade upon the enemy, which did great execution, and very much contributed to their final destruction. The troops, as soon as landed, were formed under the immediate orders of Brigadier General Pike, who led in a most gallant manner the attack upon the forts, and after having carried two redoubts in their approach to their principal works, the enemy (having previously laid a train) blew up his magazine, which in its effects upon our troops, was dreadful, having killed and wounded a great many, and amongst the former, the ever to be lamented Brigadier General Pike, who fell at the head of his column by a contusion received by a heavy stone from the magazine. His death at this time, is much to be regretted, as he had the perfect confidence of the major general; and his known activity, zeal and experience, make his loss a national one.

In consequence of the fall of general Pike, the command of the troops devolved, for a time, upon Colonel Pearce, who soon after took possession of the town. About 2 PM the American flag was substituted for the British, and at about four our troops were in quiet possession of the town. As soon as General Dearborn learned the situation of General Pike, he landed, and assumed the command. I have the honour of enclosing a copy of the capitulation which was entered into, and approved by General Dearborn and myself.

...I cannot speak in too much praise of the cool intrepidity of the officers and men generally, under my command, and I feel myself particularly indebted to the officers commanding vessels, for their zeal in seconding my views."

The remarkable account of the Fort Dearborn Massacre remains chilling 200 years after the incident and reveals the dangers all American settlers were exposed to on the edges of the western frontier. The Native American warriors of the First Nation allied with the British early in the war, hoping to defend their tribal hunting grounds from American settlement and expansion. In this case, the Potawatomi and Winnebago Indians were allied with the British and carried out a ruthlessly efficient cull of the small American force holding the frontier post of Fort Dearborn (on the site of present-day Chicago). Lieutenant Linai Helm penned this account of the massacre on August 15, 1812, for his superiors as soon as he was released by the Indians, three months later.

"...The ammunition and muskets were all destroyed the night of the 13th. The 15th, we evacuated the Garrison, and about one and half mile from the Garrison we were informed by Capt. Wells that we were surrounded and the attack by the Indians began about 10 of the clock morning. The men in a few minutes were, with the exception of 10, all killed and wounded. The Ensign and Surgeons Mate were both killed. The Capt. and myself both badly wounded during the battle. I fired my piece at an Indian and felt confident I killed him or wounded him badly. I immediately called to the men to follow me in the pirara, or we would be shot down before we could load our guns. We had proceeded under a heavy fire about an hundred and five paces when I made a wheel to the left to observe the motion of the Indians and avoid being shot in the back, which I had so far miraculously escaped. Just as I wheeled I received a ball through my coat pocket, which struck the barrel of my gun and fell in the lining of my coat. In a few seconds, I received a ball in my right foot, which lamed me considerably.

The Indians happened immediately to stop firing and never more renewed it. I immediately ordered the men that were able to load their guns and commenced loading for them that were not able. I now discovered Capt. Heald for the first time to my knowledge during the battle. He was coming from towards the Indians and to my great surprise they never offered to fire on him. He came up and ordered the men to form; that his intentions were to charge the body of Indians that were on the bank of the Lake where we had just retreated from. They appeared to be about 300 strong. We were 27, including all the wounded. He advanced about 5 steps and not at all

to my surprise was the first that halted. Some of the men fell back instead of advancing. We then gained the only high piece of ground there was near. We now had a little time to reflect and saw death in every direction.

At this time an interpreter from the Indians advanced towards us and called for the Captain, who immediately went to meet him (the interpreter was a half Indian and had lived a long time within a few yards of the fort and bound to Mr. Kinzie; he was always very friendly with us all). A chief by the name of Blackbird advanced to the interpreter and met the Captain, who after a few words conversation delivered him his sword, and in a few minutes returned to us and informed me he had offered 100 dollars for every man that was then living. He said they were then deciding on what to do. They, however, in a few minutes, called him again and talked with him some time, when he returned and informed me they had agreed if I and the men would surrender by laying down our arms they would lay down theirs, meet us half way, shake us by the hand as friends and take us back to the fort. I asked him if he knew what they intended doing with us then. He said they did not inform him. He asked me if I would surrender.

The men were at this time crowding to my back and began to beg me not to surrender. I told them not to be uneasy for I had already done my best for them and was determined not to surrender unless I saw better prospects of us all being saved and then not without they were willing. The Captain asked me the second time what I would do, without an answer. I discovered the interpreter at this time running from the Indians towards us, and when he came in about 20 steps the Captain put the question the third time. The Interpreter called out, 'Lieut. don't surrender for if you do they will kill you all, for there has been no general council held with them yet. You must wait, and I will go back and hold a general council with them and return and let you know what they will do.' I told him to go, for I had no idea of surrender. He went and collected all the Indians and talked for some time, when he returned and told me the Indians said if I would surrender as before described they would not kill any, and said it was his opinion they would do as they said, for they had already saved Mr. Kinzie and some of the women and children. This enlivened me and the men, for we well knew Mr. Kinzie stood higher than any man in that country among the Indians, and he might be the means of saving us from utter destruction, which afterwards proved to be the case.

We then surrendered, and after the Indians had fired off our guns they put the Captain and myself and some of the wounded men on horses and marched us to the bank of the lake, where the battle first commenced. When we arrived at the bank and looked down on the sand beach I was struck with horror at the sight of men, women and children lying naked with principally all their heads off, and in passing over the bodies I was confident I saw my wife with her head off about two feet from her shoulders. Tears for the first time rushed in my eyes, but I consoled myself with a firm belief that I should soon follow her.

...They attempted to strip me, but were prevented by a Chief who stuck close to me. I made signs to him that I wanted to drink, for the weather was very warm. He led me off towards the Fort and, to my great astonishment, saw my wife sitting among some squaws crying. Our feelings can be better judged than expressed. They brought some water and directed her to wash and dress my wound, which she did, and bound it up with her pocket handkerchief. They then brought up some of the men and tommyhawked one of them before us. They now took Mrs. Helm across the river (for we were nearly on its banks) to Mr. Kinzie's. We met again at my father's in the State of New York, she having arrived seven days before me after being separated seven months and one week. She was taken in the direction of Detroit and I was taken down to Illinois River and was sold to Mr. Thomas Forsyth, half brother of Mr. Kinzie's, who, a short time after, effected my escape. This gentleman was the means of saving many lives on the warring frontier. I was taken on the 15th of August and arrived safe among the Americans at St. Louis on the 14th of October."

John Richardson, a British officer in the 41st Infantry Regiment wrote to his uncle Captain Charles Askin after the battle of the River Raisin in February 1813. His letter is in two distinct parts. The first half describes a bitterly fought battle between a British force of 1,300 and a mixed American force of regular troops and militia under General Hull. The writer was horrified by the Americans' barbaric acts of firing on the wounded, but noted in grim satisfaction the British revenge on them. Of the 934 American soldiers that were engaged, only 31 survived, the rest were massacred by the First Nation Warriors, or captured. In the second half, Richardson recounts his feelings, principally his exhaustion and frustration that his musket was broken. He was overcome with drowsiness throughout the battle, a sign, perhaps that he was suffering from exposure after five day's march in the sub-zero February weather.

"Amherstburg, 4 February 1813

You have doubtless heard ere this of the engagement at the River Raisin on Friday, the 22nd inst. (ult.); however, you may probably not have heard the particulars of the business, which are simply these: On Monday, the 18th, we received information that the Americans, under the command of General Winchester, after an obstinate resistance, had driven from the River Raisin a detachment of Militia under Major Reynolds (also a party of Indians) which had been stationed there some time. That they had sustained great loss from the fire of our Indians, and from a 3-pounder, which was most ably served by Bombardier Kitson (since dead), of the R.A.

On Tuesday part of our men moved over the river to Brownstown, consisting of a Detachment of R. Artillery, with 3 3-pounders and 3 small howitzers, Capt. Tallon's Company (41st Regt.), a few Militia, and the sailors attached to the Guns. An alarm was given that the enemy were at hand. The Guns were unlimbered and everything prepared for action, when the alarm was found to be false.

On Wednesday the remainder of the army joined us at Brownstown, where (including Regulars, Militia, Artillery, Sailors and Indians) we mustered near 1,000 men. We lay, this night, at Brownstown. Next day the army commenced its march towards the River Raisin and encamped, this night, at Rocky River, which (you know) is about 12 miles beyond Brownstown and 6 on this side the River Raisin. About two hours before day we resumed our march. On Friday at daybreak we perceived the enemy's fires very distinctly—all silent in their camp. The army drew up and formed the line of battle in 2 adjoining fields, and moved down towards the enemy, the Guns advanced 20 or 30 paces in front and the Indians on our flanks. We had got tolerably near their Camp when we heard their Reveille drum beat (so completely lulled into security were they that they had not the most distant idea of an enemy being near), and soon after we heard a shot or two from the Centinels, who had by this time discovered us. Their Camp was immediately in motion. The Guns began to play away upon them at a fine rate, keeping up a constant fire.

The Americans drew up and formed behind a thick picketing, from whence they kept up a most galling fire upon our men, who, from the darkness of the morning, supposed the pickets to be the Americans; however, as it grew lighter, they discovered their mistake, and advanced within 70 or 80 paces of the pickets, but finding that scarce one of their shots took effect, as they almost all lodged in the fence. Being thus protected from the fire of our men they took a cool and deliberate aim at our Troops, who fell very fast, and the most of the men at the Guns being either killed or wounded, it was thought expedient to retire towards the enemy's left under cover of some houses.

I was a witness of a most barbarous act of inhumanity on the part of the Americans, who fired upon our poor wounded, helpless soldiers, who were endeavouring to crawl away on their hands and feet from the scene of action, and were thus tumbled over like so many hogs. However, the deaths of those brave men were avenged by the slaughter of 300 of the flower of Winchester's army, which had been ordered to turn our flanks, but who, having divided into two parties, were met, driven back, pursued, tomakawked and scalped by our Indians, (very few escaping) to carry the news of their defeat.

The General himself was taken prisoner by the Indians, with his son, aide, and several other officers. He immediately dispatched a messenger to Colonel Procter, desiring him to acquaint him with the circumstance of his being a prisoner, and to intimate that if the Colonel would send an officer to his Camp to summons the remainder of his army to surrender, he would send an order by him to his officer then commanding to surrender the Troops. Colonel Procter objected to sending one of his own officers, but permitted the General to send his aide (with a flag). The firing instantly ceased on both sides, and about 2 hours afterwards the enemy (460 in number) laid down their arms and surrendered themselves prisoners of war. A good many of our officers were wounded in the engagement, but none of them killed...

This is as accurate an account as I can give you of the Engagement. I will now give you an account of my feelings on the occasion. When we first drew up in the field I was ready to fall down with fatigue from marching and carrying a heavy musquet. Even when the balls were flying about my ears as thick as hail I felt quite drowsy and sleepy, and, indeed, I was altogether in a very disagreeable dilemma.

The night before at Rocky River, some one or other of the men took my firelock and left his own in the place. It being quite dark when we set out from that place, I could not distinguish one from another. Enquiry was vain, so I was obliged to take the other (without thinking that anything was the matter with it). When we came to the firing part of the business I could not get my gun off. It flashed in the pan, and I procured a wire and worked away at it with that. I tried it again, and again it flashed. I never was so vexed-to think that I was exposed to the torrent of fire from the enemy without having the power to return a single shot quite disconcerted the economy of my pericranium; though if I had fired fifty rounds not one of them would have had any effect, except upon the pickets, which I was not at all ambitious of assailing like another Don Quixote.

Our men had fired 4 or 5 rounds when I was called to assist my brother Robert, who was wounded, and who fell immediately, and which led me to suppose that he was mortally wounded. However, when he was carried to the doctors I found the poor fellow had escaped with a broken leg, which torments him very much, and it will be some time before he gets over it. I think it is highly probable we shall have a brush with the valiant Harrison, who is said to be at the Rapids of the Miami River, or near them. If so, I think we shall have tight work, as we have lost in killed and wounded in the action of the 22nd 180 men (exclusive of Indians).

Pray remember me to my cousins."

Washington was not strategically important, but the British decided to attack the young republic's capital both to create a diversion from campaigns elsewhere and as retaliation for the destruction of York and Port Dover. The American Secretary of War, John Armstrong, was concentrating his forces on the defense of Baltimore and panicked when British troops landed in Chesapeake Bay. American defensive measures were almost laughable, as amateur American militia clashed with veteran British soldiers. The British managed to destroy the seat of the American government, the White House and the House of Representatives, and burned the entire capital in a humiliating assault.

Thomas Tingey's letter to the Secretary of War is a verbose and pompous account of events. Charged with destroying the naval yard, Tingey is clearly intent on salvaging his reputation (and his possessions), afraid that he may be blamed in some way. Compared with the spare yet illuminating prose of so many military commanders, Tingey's letter seems simply craven and overblown. Nevertheless, it is an excellent eyewitness account of a period of confusion and destruction at the heart of American government.

"Navy Yard, Washington, 27 August 1814

After receiving your orders of the 24th, directing the public shipping, stores, &c. at this establishment, to be destroyed, in case of the success of the enemy over our army, no time was lost in making the necessary arrangements for firing the whole, and preparing boats for departing from the yard, as you had suggested. About 4 PM I received a message by an officer, from the Secretary of War, with information that he could 'protect me no longer.' Soon after this, I was informed that the conflagration of the Eastern Branch bridge had commenced; and, in a few minutes, the explosion announced the blowing up of that part near the 'draw,' as had been arranged in the morning.

It had been promulgated, as much as in my power, among the inhabitants of the vicinity, the intended fate of the yard, in order that they might take every possible precaution for the safety of themselves, families, and property. Immediately several individuals came, in succession, endeavoring to prevail on me to deviate from my instructions, which they were invariably informed was unavailing, unless they could bring me your instructions in writing, countermanding those previously given. A deputation also of the most respectable women came on the same errand, when I found myself painfully necessitated to inform them that any farther importunities would cause the matches to be instantly applied to the trains, with

Above left: The burning of Washington D.C. by British troops, 1814.

Left: The ill-fated British attack on the *General Armstrong* in Fayal Harbor, the Azores, 1814, a hand-tinted print by Nathaniel Currier in the 1830s. The unprovoked storming of the *General Armstrong* became something of a legend in America, the heroism of her captain, Samuel C. Reid, inspiring popular songs, poetry, and paintings.

assurance, however, that if left at peace, I would delay the execution of the orders as long as I could feel the least shadow of justification. Captain Creighton's arrival at the yard, with the men who had been with him at the bridge, (probably about 5 o'clock,) would have justified me in instant operation; but he also was strenuous in the desire to obviate the intended destruction, and volunteered to ride out and gain me positive information, as to the position of the enemy, under the hope that our army might have rallied and repulsed them. I was myself, indeed, desirous of delay, for the reason that the wind was then blowing fresh from the south-south-west, which would most probably have caused the destruction of all the private property north and east of the yard, in its neighbourhood. I was of opinion, also, that the close of the evening would bring with it a calm, in which happily we were not disappointed. Other gentlemen, well mounted, volunteered, as Captain Creighton had done, to go out and bring me positive intelligence of the enemy's situation, if possible to obtain it.

The evening came, and I waited with much anxiety the return of captain Creighton, having almost continual information that the enemy were in the neighbourhood of the marine barracks,—at the capitol hill—and that their 'advance' was near Georgetown... It had been my intention not to leave the vicinity of the yard with my boat during the night; but having captain Creighton and other gentlemen with me, she was too much encumbered and overladen to render that determination proper. We therefore proceeded to Alexandria, in the vicinity of which I rested till the morning of the 25th, when, having also refreshed the gig's crew, we left Alexandria at half past 7 o'clock, and proceeded again up to the yard, where I landed, unmolested, about a quarter before nine.

... The detail issuing store of the navy store keeper had remained safe from the fire during the night, which the enemy, (being in force in the yard) about 8 o'clock set fire to, and it was speedily consumed. It appeared that they had left the yard about half an hour when we arrived. I found my dwelling house, and that of Lieutenant Haraden, untouched by fire; but some of the people of the neighbourhood had recommenced plundering them; therefore, hastily collecting a few persons known to me, I got some of my most valuable materials moved to neighbours' houses out of the yard, who tendered me their offers to receive them, the enemy's officers having declared private property sacred.

Could I have staid another hour, I had probably saved all my furniture and stores; but being advised by some friends, that I was not safe, they believing that the admiral was by that time, or would speedily be informed of my being in the yard, he having expressed an anxious desire to make me captive, but had said that the officers' dwellings in the yard should not be destroyed. I therefore again embarked in the gig, taking along out of the branch one of the new launches, which lay safe, although along side of a floating stage enveloped in flames. I had no sooner gone than such a scene of devastation and plunder took place in the houses (by the people of the neighbourhood,) as is disgraceful to relate; not a moveable article, from the cellars to the garrets, has been left us, and even some of the fixtures, and the locks of the doors, have been shamefully pillaged. Some of the perpetrators, however, have been made known to me.

From the number and movements of the enemy, it would have appeared rash temerity to have attempted returning again that day, though my inclination strongly urged it; therefore, reconnoitering their motions, as well as could be effected at a convenient distance in the gig, until evening, I again proceeded to Alexandria for the night. Yesterday morning, the 26th, it was impossible to form (from the various and contradictory reports at Alexandria) any sort of probable conjecture, either of the proceedings and situation of our army, or that of the enemy. Determining, therefore, to have a positive knowledge of some part thereof, from ocular demonstration, I again embarked in the gig, proceeding with due caution to the yard, where I learned with chagrin the devastation and pillage before mentioned, and found also, to my surprise, that the old gun boat, which had been loaded with provisions, and had grounded, in endeavouring to get out of the branch, on the evening of the 24th, was nearly discharged of her cargo, by a number of our people, without connexion with each other. Having landed in the yard, I soon ascertained that the enemy had left the city, excepting only a serjeant's guard, for the security of the sick and wounded. Finding it impracticable to stop the scene of plunder that had commenced, I determined instantly on repossessing the yard, with all the force at my command. Repairing, therefore, immediately to Alexandria, Lieutenant Haraden, the ordinary men, and the few marines there, were ordered directly up; following myself, I got full possession again at evening."

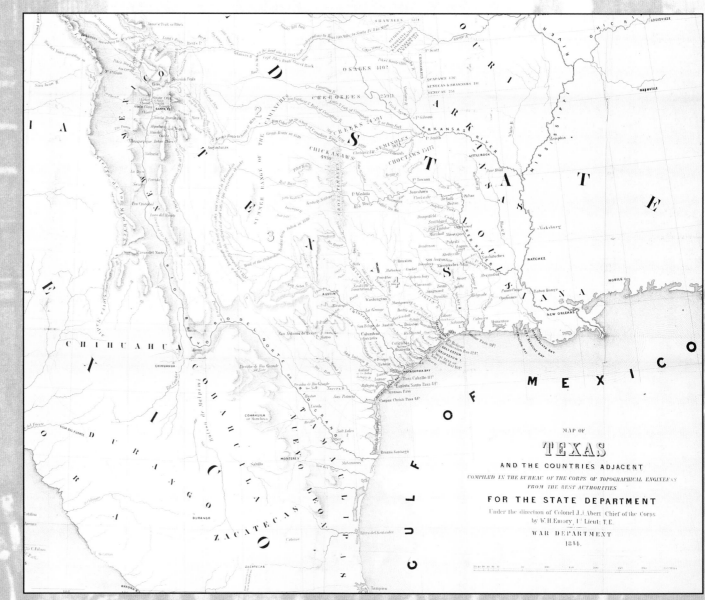

MAP OF

TEXAS

AND THE COUNTRIES ADJACENT

COMPILED IN THE BUREAU OF THE CORPS OF TOPOGRAPHICAL ENGINEERS
FROM THE BEST AUTHORITIES

FOR THE STATE DEPARTMENT

Under the direction of Colonel J.J. Abert, Chief of the Corps
by W.H. Emory, 1st Lieut: T.E.

WAR DEPARTMENT
1844.

Right: A map of Texas in 1844. At this time Texas was an independent state. It was only to join the Union, as the 28th state, on December 29, 1845.

Far right: Known as "Old Fuss and Feathers" because of his rigorous enforcement of discipline and uniform, General Winfield Scott (1786–1866) was commander of the U.S. army for 20 years, 1841–1861.

Frontier Wars 1815–1860

One of the long-lasting effects of the War of 1812 was that America turned inward. Having persuaded Britain that the U.S.A. was not an offshoot of Europe, the country took very little part in European affairs for the rest of the 19th century and concentrated on expanding and consolidating the western frontiers.

Between 1820 and 1830, about 20,000 Americans settled in Texas, which was then the northern province of Mexico, and they were initially welcomed by the Mexican government. Over time, however, the settlers began to agitate for self-determination, protesting against the Mexican government's religious laws and proscriptions against slave owning. In 1835, the Mexicans attempted to impose order on the unruly settlers by garrisoning the province with troops, who inevitably clashed with the settlers. General Santa Anna, the president of Mexico led a 6,000-strong force to the Alamo, an abandoned mission fortified by the Texans and manned by 183 men, including the famous frontiersmen Davy Crockett and Jim Bowie. Outnumbered and outgunned, the Texans withstood a ten-day siege before they were overpowered on March 6, 1836. All the Texans perished, but Mexican losses were an astonishing 1,500.

"To: Unknown
From: George C. Childers—Washington, Brazos, Tx.
Date: April 16, 1836—The Kentucky Republican—Hopkinsville, Ky

Dear Sir:

The unpleasant intelligence has just reached this place, by express, from the commander-in-chief, on the western frontier, that a renewed attack was made, on Sunday morning, the 6th inst., led by Santa Ana, in person—that previous to the attack, the Mexican

Above: Monterrey was a fortified town garrisoned by 10,000 Mexican troops. General Zachary Taylor launched an attack on September 21, 1846.

Jefferson Davis (president of the Confederate states, 1861–1865) served as colonel of the 1st Mississippi Rifles in Mexico and distinguished himself at the battle of Buena Vista on February 27, 1847. This rather breathless letter to his brother Joseph E. Davis was written after the Battle of Monterrey, although his hope that the war was over, was rather optimistic.

"Monter[r]ey Sept. 25th, 1846.

My Dear Brother
The town is ours after a severe conflict. The Mississippians were brought into action on the 21st and performed some brilliant service. On the 22nd preparations were made, and we held an advance post. On the morning of the 23rd we (the Mississippians) opened the action early, and continued firing and advancing into the town until near sunset, when we were ordered to withdraw. On the 24th propositions having been received to capitulate, Gen. Worth, and Gen. Henderson of Texas, and myself, were appointed commissioners to arrange the terms of capitulation. We agreed, and the papers have

been exchanged. It was reported to us, by the Mexican General, that Mexico had received commissioners from the United States.

They were whipped, and we could afford to be generous. We hope soon to return as the war is probably over.

With love to all—I am your brother."

Thomas J. Jackson, later known as "Stonewall," was a lieutenant in a light artillery company, and as he rather ruefully noted in an earlier letter, "I belong to a company of light Artillery which is frequently called flying artillery. In an action if all the officers of the company should be well, I will have to carry dispatches being unfortunately too low to have a command." He arrived in Mexico in September 1846 as part of General Winfield Scott's army. Jackson was a devout Episcopalian, and found Mexico to be quite foreign and strange; he was amazed by the highly decorated churches, and rather disparaging about the Catholic beliefs of the people, which he referred to as "superstitions." He was a reliable correspondent, and his letters to his sister not only provide wonderful descriptions of the country, but also something of his own living conditions: he refers to using a box as a writing table and remarks on the frequency of the post.

Above: After four days of bloody hand-to-hand combat, the Mexicans requested a truce.

"March 30 1847
Camp near Vera Cruz, Mexico

Dear Sister

I now send you the long delayed letter and hope that you will pardon my procrastination since I last wrote to you. I have been at Matamoras Camargo Monterey and Saltillo and the intermediate towns. At present I can not conveniently give you a general idea of the portions of Mexico which have fallen under my observation but hope to do so at some future day when things are more settled than at present and I also purpose on writing to you more frequently.

It would have [afforded] me much pleasure to have been with the gallant and victorious General Taylor at the battle of Buena Vista in which he has acquired laurels as imperishable as the history which shall record the invasion of Mexico by our victorious armies. But I was ordered away from Saltillo in January last and I believe for the best inasmuch as I am now with the most important portion of the army and on the most important line of operations.

I am now encamped on the road leading from Vera Cruz to the city of Mexico. Our troops landed about two miles from the former city on the ninth inst and on the same night were fired on by the Mexicans. On the following day we commenced surrounding the city and operating against it. The operations after the [investment] was completed consisted principally in bombarding and cannonading which were continued until not only the city but the castle of San Juan Dulloa agreed to surrender. The capitulation occurred yesterday. The terms are that all the public property falls into our hands, the troops march out under the condition of not serving against us during the present war unless exchanged. The troops marched out yesterday and surrendered their arms and we took possession immediately. This capitulation has thrown into our hands the strong hold of this republic and being a regular [siege] in connection with other circumstances must in my opinion excel any military operations known in the history of our country. I approve of all except allowing the enemy to retire that I can not approve of in as much as we had them secure and could have taken them prisoners of war unconditionally.

Our loss is not accurately known nor that of the enemy either yet but in my estimation ours can not exceed twenty men in killed, we lost only two captains (Capt Vinton of the artillery and Capt Alburtis of the infantry). I have been in the city and was much surprised at its strength. It is surrounded on the land side by a wall about 10 feet high and a series of forts and on the other side is protected by the castle.

You asked me whether I belonged to General Worth's division. I had the honor of being in it so long as it existed but it has been broken up during the past siege. I was part of the time with him and part of the time with General Twigs. Whilst I was at the advanced batteries a cannon ball came in about five steps of me. I presume that you think my name ought to appear in the papers but when you come to consider the composition of our army you will entertain different views. Its composition is such that those who have independent commands only are as a general rule spoken of for instance Ridgely May [Bra—] Duncan Ringold Smith all commanded companies. If an officer wishes to distinguish himself he must remain long in service until he obtains rank then he obtains the praise not only for his efforts but for the efforts of the officers and men under him. That portion of praise which may be due to me must of course go to those above me or be included in the praise given to the army.

My health is extremely good. I probably look better than I have for years. I expect to remain in Mexico for the remainder of the war and expect to move forward with the leading Brigade. I expect to be promoted in a short time to a second lieutenancy. This will probably occasion me to leave the light battery but it will give me more rank which is of the greatest importance in the army.

Remember me in the warmest terms to Mr. Arnold and all my other friends. I rejoice at your prosperity and hope and doubt not that it will continue. I hope soon to march forward towards the city of Mexico. Vera Cruz continues healthy. I intend writing soon and more frequently as my feelings incline me to and as a brother ought. Your last letters coming in such quick succession served as a just rebuke but my means for writing are poor. Even now I am using a box for a chair and my camp bedstead as a writing desk and think myself comfortably situated. You have all the conveniences necessary and I hope that you will use them to write often to one who esteems you above all."

Left: In August 1847 Scott began to advance on Mexico City. The Mexicans took up a well-defended position at Churubusco.

"Jalapa Mexico
April 22d 1847
Dear Sister

I promised in my last that I would give you a more detailed account of Mexico in a subsequent letter. I will now endeavor to comply with that promise. In doing so I will first state in general terms that the portion of Northern Mexico which has fallen under my observation is mostly a vast barren waste cities excepted. There are but two seasons in Mexico wet & dry. In consequence of the drought there is but little vegetation in the north. A person in traveling through this sterile portion of country would not suppose that the country inhabitants were able to pay their taxes. But in the cities it is different. There wealth is frequently found one person residing in Saltillo is said to own a larger area of land than the state of New York...

About 50 miles farther west is Saltillo the capital of Coahuila. Its [height] is about 2000 feet above the level of Monterey on an inclined plane at the edge of the table lands. The houses are generally built of sun dried brick as are most of the houses in that region. The church is the most highly ornamented on the interior of any edifice which has ever come under my observation. On entering this magnificent structure we are struck with the gaudy appearance on every side but most especially the opposite end which appears to be gilded with gold. At the bottom is a magnificent silver altar and on each side are statues which can not fail to attract the attention of the astonished beholder. The music is of the highest character. The priests are robed in the most gaudy of apparel. The inhabitants take off their hats on approaching the church and do not replace them until past it. One day whilst I was near the building I observed a señora (lady) gradually approaching the door on another occasion I saw a female looking at a statue and weeping like a child. Such is the superstition of this race.

After obtaining a [limited] transportation for General Twigg's division it set forward for Jalapa on the road leading to the city of Mexico. But on arriving near Cerro Gordo we learned that General Santa Anna held the pass in force consequently we waited for reinforcements which finally arrived and on the 17 Inst we attacked the Mexicans but did not succeed in routing them completely until the 18th when we took some thousand prisoners and completely routed the remainder. We followed close on the retreating column until night and came near enough to give the retreating enemy a few shots from the battery. But they succeeded in effecting their escape for

want of our dragoons. General Scott after disarming the prisoners allowed them to retire the officers on [parole]. But General La Vega who is again our prisoner refused to except of his and I presume that he will be sent back to the U.S. Our loss has been considerable but not known neither is the Mexican. General Santa Anna escaped but in his haste left us his carriage & together with some thousand dollars in specie...

I can say no more as I have just learned that the escort by which I wish to send this has started because I must mount my horse & over take it or miss a good opportunity. I am in better health than usual.

[unsigned]"

Left: The bombardment of Veracruz by American troops, 1847.

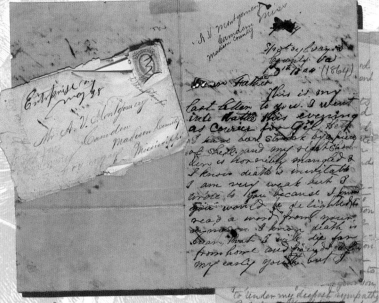

Right: A selection of original letters from the Civil War.

Far right: An 1863 portrait of Abraham Lincoln, the 16th president of the United States.

The American Civil War 1861–1865

The Civil War was America's most divisive conflict, and its impact on the country's history was enormous. A nation proud of its unity only 50 short years before was ripped in two, families were polarized, and many were split by their beliefs. It is not surprising that this calamitous event yielded a wealth of correspondence. Families unaffected by the fighting were rare, and the sudden change to the lifestyles of young men—insular country boys dragged away from their farms, or hard-working young office clerks or tradesmen—was shocking and cataclysmic for them all. It was made all the more dreadful by the fact that Americans were not facing a common enemy against whom they could feel jingoistic righteousness, but they were facing their own countrymen.

The war was caused by the different economic and political outlooks of the Northern and Southern States. The North—those states north of Washington D.C.—was an industrialized society of some 26 million souls, while the South was an agrarian economy dependent upon slave labor for the production of cotton and tobacco, its staple crops. The population of the South was 9 million—3 million of whom were slaves and unavailable for military service. The election of the republican president, Abraham Lincoln, in 1860, brought matters to a head. Lincoln and his party favored the abolition of slavery and his rise to power heralded the Secession from the Union of southern states terrified by the prospect of social, and thus economic, change.

Many factors favored the North: it housed the financial and industrial centers of America and the sheer numbers of its population meant that enlistment to the armed forces would not be a problem. The South was far poorer, but enjoyed substantial geographical advantages: the sheer size of the area, for example, and the fact that much of the landscape was little more than wilderness seriously hindered Union communications.

With hindsight, it seems that neither side quite believed that the rupture of the Union would really lead to war. Lincoln referred to hostilities as an "insurrection" in April 1861 and few predicted that the war would last four

Above: Robert E. Lee (1807–1870), commander of the Confederate forces.

long and bloody years and affect over a million men, who were either killed or wounded.

The Civil War has been called the first modern war, principally because civilian society was for the first time in the front line of battle, starved or shelled into submission as part of a sustained campaign. And even if they were lucky enough to escape that fate, the new science of photography as practiced by Matthew Brady and his assistants brought the images of war to a wider public with a brutal clarity. Furthermore, a large percentage of the population was now literate and could write home, telling their families exactly what they were experiencing. A great many letters still survive, written by civilian men who had suddenly been catapulted into uniform.

By 1865, the whole country realized that they had participated in a momentous war, and it was partly because of this immediate awareness that the current events of the 1860s would impact so strongly upon history, that so many letters, dispatches, and memoirs of the era survive. Written by men and women from all walks of life and of every military rank, they make the Civil War accessible and immediate almost 150 years after its end.

The generals of the opposing forces in the Civil War knew each other well —many had served together in the Mexican War 13 years earlier, or had studied at the military academy at West Point—and this familiarity with their opponents was an unusual facet of the war. Robert E. Lee, the commander of the Confederate forces, had a long and distinguished career in the U.S. Army before he felt driven by his loyalty to his state to resign his commission in 1861. This letter to his son, written in January 1861, reflects the feelings of many Southern soldiers.

"The South, in my opinion, had been aggravated by the acts of the North... As an American citizen I... would defend any State if her rights were invaded. But I can anticipate no greater calamity for the country than a dissolution of the Union. It would be an accumulation of all the evils we complain of, and I am willing to sacrifice everything but honor for its preservation.

...Still a Union that can only be maintained by swords and bayonets, and in which strife and civil war take the place of brotherly love and kindness has no charm for me... if the Union is dissolved and the government disrupted, I shall return to my native State and share the miseries of my people, and save in defense will draw my sword on none."

On February 7, the Southern states seceded from the Union and united as the Confederate States of America. On April 13, Fort Sumter fell to Confederate forces after a 32-hour bombardment and four days later President Lincoln asked Lee to take command of the Union forces. This helped Lee to clarify his position and six days later, with much regret, he resigned his commission in the United States Army.

"To General Winfield Scott
Commander-in-Chief, United States Army
Arlington, Washington City P.O.
April 20, 1861

General:
Since my interview with you on the 18th instant I have felt that I ought not longer to retain my commission in the Army. I therefore tender my resignation, which I request you will recommend for acceptance.

It would have been presented at once, but for the struggle it has cost me to separate myself from a service to which I have devoted all the best years of my life & all the ability I possessed.

During the whole of that time, more than 30 years, I have experienced nothing but kindness from my superiors, & the most cordial friendship from my companions. To no one Genl have I been as much indebted as to yourself for uniform kindness & consideration, & it has always been my ardent desire to merit your approbation.

I shall carry with me to the grave the most grateful recollections of your kind consideration, & your name & fame will always be dear to me. Save in the defence of my native State, I never desire again to draw my sword.

Be pleased to accept my most earnest wishes for the continuance of your happiness & prosperity & believe me most truly yours

Robert E. Lee"

Two days later, loyalty to the Confederate caused him to accept the post of commander of the Confederate army.

Like Lee, Pierre Gustave Toussant Beauregard, a French Creole from Louisiana, was also a career soldier. In January 1861 he was appointed Superintendent of the U.S. Military Academy at West Point but resigned five

Above: Pierre Gustave Beauregard (1818–1893), a Confederate brigadier general who led the attack on Fort Sumter, South Carolina.

days later (and still has the distinction of being the superintendent with shortest term of office). Almost instantly, he became a Confederate brigadier general and in March was sent to Charleston, South Carolina, where he led the attack on Fort Sumter. Immediately after it was over, he sent this dispatch to Jefferson Davis, president of the Confederacy.

"Sir: I have the honor to submit the following summary statement of the circumstances of the surrender of Fort Sumter: On the refusal of Major Anderson to engage, in compliance with my demand, to designate the time when he would evacuate Fort Sumter, and to agree meanwhile not to use his guns against us, at 3:20 o'clock in the morning of the 12th instant I gave him formal notice that within one hour my batteries would open on him. In consequence of some circumstance of delay the bombardment was not begun precisely at the appointed moment, but at 4:30 o'clock the signal gun was fired, and within twenty minutes all our batteries were in full play. There was no response from Fort Sumter until about 7 o'clock, when the first shot from the enemy was discharged against our batteries on Cummings Point.

By 8 o'clock the action became general, and throughout the day was maintained by spirit on both sides. Our guns were served with skill and energy. The effect was visible in the impressions made on the walls of Fort Sumter. From our mortar batteries shells were thrown with such precision and rapidity that it soon became impossible for the enemy to employ his gun "en barbette," of which several were dismounted. The engagement was continued without any circumstance of special note until night fall before which time the fire from Sumter had evidently slackened. Operations on our side were sustained through' out the night, provoking, however, only a feeble response.

On the morning of the 13th the action was prosecuted with renewed vigor, and about 7:30 o'clock it was discovered our shells had set fire to the barracks in the fort. Speedily volumes of smoke indicated an extensive conflagration, and apprehending some terrible calamity to the garrison, I immediately dispatched an offer of assistance to Major Anderson which, however, with grateful acknowledgments, he declined. Meanwhile, being informed about 2 o'clock that a white flag was displayed from Sumter, I dispatched two of my aides to Major Anderson with terms of evacuation. In recognition of the gallantry exhibited by the garrison I cheerfully agreed that on surrendering the fort the commanding officer might salute his flag.

By 8 o'clock the terms of evacuation were definitely accepted. Major Anderson having expressed a desire to communicate with the United States vessels lying off the harbor, with a view to arranging for the transportation of his command to some port in the United States, one of his officers, accompanied by Captain Hartstene and three of my aides, was permitted to visit the officer in command of the squadron to make provision for that object. Because of an unavoidable delay the formal transfer of the fort to our possession did not take place until 4 o'clock in the afternoon of the 14th instant. At that hour, the place having been evacuated by the United States garrison, our troops occupied it, and the Confederate flag was hoisted on the ramparts of Sumter with a salute from the various batteries.

The steamer 'Isabel' having been placed at the service of Major Anderson, he and his command were transferred to the United States vessels off the harbor...

I remain, sir, very respectfully, your obedient servant,

P. G. T. Beauregard,
Brigadier-General, Commanding,
Headquarters Provisional Army, C. S. A.,
Charleston, S. C.,
April 16, 1861."

With the fall of Fort Sumter, Union sensibilities were inflamed and there was a rush of men to the recruiting offices. Lincoln called for 42,000 volunteers to serve the army of the North for three years, or the duration of the war and each state immediately raised volunteer regiments who poured into Washington to await orders.

On July 21, 1861, the Northern commander, General Irvin McDowell led an army of 28,452 men to Bull Run Creek, near Manassas to meet some 21,000 Confederates under Beauregard, the hero of Fort Sumter. Although the Union forces launched a vigorous attack, they were stopped in their tracks by a determined response from "Stonewall" Jackson's troops, and were further beaten back by some 10,000 reinforcements under Joseph E.

Johnston. McDowell had the dubious honor of presiding over the union's first battle, which was little short of a rout for the North, and he was replaced as commander by George B. McClellan.

The first Union army was a disparate, inexperienced force, full of righteous northern patriotism, but short on discipline and battle skills. It was a volunteer force, however, so individuals were very sure of why they were fighting as the following missive, the last letter of Sullivan Ballou, shows. Ballou, was a 32-year-old major in the 2nd Rhode Island Volunteers and had recently qualified as a lawyer. His beautifully written letter, at once an apologia for his beliefs and a love letter to his wife, has become one of the most famous letters of the war.

"Washington, D.C., 14 July 1861

My very dear Sarah:

The indications are very strong that we shall move in a few days—perhaps tomorrow. Lest I should not be able to write you again, I feel impelled to write lines that may fall under your eye when I shall be no more.

Our movement may be one of a few days duration and full of pleasure—and it may be one of severe conflict and death to me. Not my will, but thine 0 God, be done. If it is necessary that I should fall on the battlefield for my country, I am ready. I have no misgivings about, or lack of confidence in, the cause in which I am engaged, and my courage does not halt or falter. I know how strongly American Civilization now leans upon the triumph of the Government, and how great a debt we owe to those who went before us through the blood and suffering of the Revolution. And I am willing—perfectly willing—to lay down all my joys in this life, to help maintain this Government, and to pay that debt.

But, my dear wife, when I know that with my own joys I lay down nearly all of yours, and replace them in this life with cares and sorrows—when, after having eaten for long years the bitter fruit of orphanage myself, I must offer it as their only sustenance to my dear little children—is it weak or dishonorable, while the banner of my purpose floats calmly and proudly in the breeze, that my unbounded love for you, my darling wife and children, should struggle in fierce, though useless, contest with my love of country?

Above: An austere man of conviction, and an outstanding military tactician, "Stonewall" Jackson (1824–1863) was one of the greatest Confederate generals.

I cannot describe to you my feelings on this calm summer night, when two thousand men are sleeping around me, many of them enjoying the last, perhaps, before that of death—and I, suspicious that Death is creeping behind me with his fatal dart, am communing with God, my country, and thee.

I have sought most closely and diligently, and often in my breast, for a wrong motive in thus hazarding the happiness of those I loved and I could not find one. A pure love of my country and of the principles have often advocated before the people and "the name of honor that I love more than I fear death" have called upon me, and I have obeyed.

Sarah, my love for you is deathless, it seems to bind me to you with mighty cables that nothing but Omnipotence could break; and yet my love of Country comes over me like a strong wind and bears me irresistibly on with all these chains to the battlefield.

The memories of the blissful moments I have spent with you come creeping over me, and I feel most gratified to God and to you that I have enjoyed them so long. And hard it is for me to give them up and burn to ashes the hopes of future years, when God willing, we might still have lived and loved together and seen our sons grow up to honorable manhood around us. I have, I know, but few and small claims upon Divine Providence, but something whispers to me—perhaps it is the wafted prayer of my little Edgar—that I shall return to my loved ones unharmed. If I do not, my dear Sarah, never forget how much I love you, and when my last breath escapes me on the battlefield, it will whisper your name.

Forgive my many faults, and the many pains I have caused you. How thoughtless and foolish I have oftentimes been! How gladly would I wash out with my tears every little spot upon your happiness, and struggle with all the misfortune of this world, to shield you and my children from harm. But I cannot. I must watch you from the spirit land and hover near you, while you buffet the storms with your precious little freight, and wait with sad patience till we meet to part no more.

But, O Sarah! If the dead can come back to this earth and flit unseen around those they loved, I shall always be near you; in the garish day and in the darkest night—amidst your happiest scenes and gloomiest hours—always, always; and if there be a soft breeze upon your cheek, it shall be my breath; or the cool air fans your throbbing temple, it shall be my spirit passing by.

Sarah, do not mourn me dead; think I am gone and wait for thee, for we shall meet again.

As for my little boys, they will grow as I have done, and never know a father's love and care. Little Willie is too young to remember me long, and my blue-eyed Edgar will keep my frolics with him among the dimmest memories of his childhood. Sarah, I have unlimited confidence in your maternal care and your development of their characters. Tell my two mothers his and hers I call God's blessing upon them. O Sarah, I wait for you there! Come to me, and lead thither my children.

Sullivan"

Facing Sullivan Ballou in the Confederate lines was Henry Campbell, a Virginia shoemaker who served for three months with the Rockridge Rifles, a unit of the 5th Virginia Infantry Regiment. He was discharged shortly after the battle, suffering from tuberculosis—possibly the sickness he refers to in the first paragraph. He certainly does not spare his mother the details of the battle, and writes with rather grim satisfaction of the injuries they inflicted on the Yankees.

"Camp at Manassas 10 o'clock p.m.
July 21st

Dear Mother,

According to promise I will attempt to give you a faint description of what I witnessed since I left home. I got to Staunton about 12 o'clock on Friday night. I was very sick at Staunton and had to stay until this morning. I came down to this place today.

They have been fighting from sunrise until Sunset today. About 12000 of the Yankees were killed. Our loss is estimated at 3 or 4,000, our company fared rather badly. Asbury McClure was killed. He died in the arms of Sandy Gordon and James Gillock. Joel Neff, Jno Moody, Preston Davidson & Charley Rollins were wounded, and

Miller was wounded mortally. Moody and Davidson were wounded in the shoulder. Charley was knocked down by a piece of shell and cut on the head, he is not hurt much just a small cut on his head, he is sitting by me laughing and talking now, it does not prevent him from going about at all, it will not unfit him for duty. Tom Rollins came out unhurt, Joe Neff is wounded in the hand. Tell Mrs. McCown that Mac came out unhurt. Our regiment drove the Yankees back at the point of the bayonet. Joe Neff knocked a Yankee's brains out with the butt of his gun.

I do not know whether any more of the company are hurt. I have not seen the main body of the company. Lieut. Lewis & Edmondson are safe, also Horace Wallace. About 50,000 of the Yankees were engaged, about 30000 of our force. We took 6 pieces of Rifled Cannon. General Patterson has been taken prisoner.

I expect I will be home in 3 or 4 days. Capt. White's company were in the fight and none were killed as far as I can hear. Capt.

White's Liberty Hall Vols. had one killed, Paxton, and 3 wounded. Bell of his company was mortally wounded. I have not seen Tom or Jerry Kelly. All of the Regulars of the Yankees were engaged today.

It is an awful sight to see the wounded and the dead. I supposed both sides will bury their dead tomorrow. I want to bring all of our wounded and dead home if I can. Our company was awfully cut up. The 2d South Carolina and 2d Mississippians were cut all to pieces.

Let Marion Parent read this letter and tell him it will have to answer for the one I promised to write. I will write tomorrow if I can.

Your affectionate Son,

R. H. Campbell"

Above: Confederate forces charge Cemetery Hill on July 2, 1863, during the Battle of Gettysburg.

McClellan embarked on the mighty task of training his army and building it into an effective fighting force—indeed Lincoln felt that he spent too long on the training, when he could have been attacking the Rebels. During 1862, he tried to impose several deadlines in an effort to get McClellan and his troops moving. It was not until McClellan was relieved of overall command of Union forces in March (retaining his post as commander of the Army of the Potomac) that he led his troops south to the peninsula between the James and York rivers in Virginia. The Peninsular Campaign was characterized by daring acts of great tactical skill by Confederate commanders such as "Stonewall" Jackson, and overcautious timidity from McClellan. Finally, after the battle of Antietam, in which Union forces enjoyed a 2:1 advantage but failed to take the initiative, and losses on both sides were the most costly of the war, Lincoln felt moved to write to McClellan, laying out in painfully simple terms how to exploit his resources.

"Executive Mansion,
Washington, D.C., October 13, 1862.

Major-General McClellan

My Dear Sir,
You remember my speaking to you of what I called your overcautiousness. Are you not overcautious when you assume that you cannot do what the enemy is constantly doing? Should you not claim to be at least his equal in prowess, and act upon the claim?

As I understand, you telegraphed General Halleck that you cannot subsist your army at Winchester unless the railroad from Harper's Ferry to that point be put in working order. But the enemy does now subsist his army at Winchester, at a distance nearly twice as great from railroad transportation as you would have to do, without the railroad last named. He now wagons from Culpeper Court-House, which is just about twice as far as you would have to do from Harper's Ferry. He is certainly not more than half as well provided with wagons as you are.

I certainly should be pleased for you to have the advantage of the railroad from Harper's Ferry to Winchester, but it wastes all the remainder of autumn to give it to you, and in fact ignores the question of time, which cannot and must not be ignored. Again, one of the standard maxims of war, as you know, is to 'operate upon the enemy's communications as much as possible without exposing your own.' You scent to act as if this applies against you, but cannot apply in your favor. Change positions with the enemy, and think you not he would break your communication with Richmond within the next twenty-four hours You dread his going into Pennsylvania, but if he does so in full force, he gives up his communications to you absolutely, and you have nothing to do but to follow and ruin him. If he does so with less than full force, fall upon and beat what is left behind all the easier. Exclusive of the water-line, you are now nearer Richmond than the enemy is by the route that you can and he must take. Why can you not reach there before him, unless you admit that he is more than your equal on a march? His route is the arc of a circle, while yours is the chord. The roads are as good on yours as on his. You know I desired, but did not order, you to cross the Potomac below instead of above the Shenandoah and Blue Ridge. My idea was that this would at once menace the enemy's communications, which I would seize if he would permit.

If he should move northward I would follow him closely, holding his communications. If he should prevent our seizing his communications and move toward Richmond, I would press closely to him; fight him, if a favorable opportunity should present, and at least try to beat him to Richmond on the inside track. I say "try;" if we never try we shall never succeed. If he makes a stand at Winchester, moving neither north nor south, I would fight him there, on the idea that if we cannot beat him when he bears the wastage of coming to us, we never can when we bear the wastage of going to him. This proposition is a simple truth, and is too important to be lost sight of for a moment. In coming to us he tenders us an advantage which we should not waive. We should not so operate as to merely drive him away. As we must beat him somewhere or fail finally, we can do it, if at all, easier near to us than far away. If we cannot beat the enemy where he now is, we never can, he again being within the intrenchments of Richmond.

Recurring to the idea of going to Richmond on the inside track, the facility of supplying from the side away from the enemy is remarkable, as it were, by the different spokes of a wheel extending from the hub toward the rim, and this, whether you move directly by the chord or on the inside arc, hugging the Blue Ridge more closely. The chord-line, as you see, carries you by Aldie, Hay Market, and Fredericksburg; and you see how turnpikes, railroads, and finally the Potomac, by Aquia Creek, meet you at all points from Washington; the same, only the lines lengthened a little, if you press closer to the Blue Ridge part of the way.

The gaps through the Blue Ridge I understand to be about the following distances from Harper's Ferry, to wit: Vestal's, 5 miles; Gregory's, 13; Snicker's, 18; Ashby's, 28; Manassas, 38; Chester, 45; and Thornton's, 53. I should think it preferable to take the route nearest the enemy, disabling him to make an important move without your knowledge, and compelling him to keep his forces together for dread of you. The gaps would enable you to attack if you should wish. For a great part of the way you would be practically between the enemy and both Washington and Richmond, enabling us to spare you the greatest number of troops from here. When at length running for Richmond ahead of him enables him to move this way, if he does so, turn and attack him in the rear. But I think he should be engaged long before such point is reached. It is all easy if our troops march as well as the enemy, and it is unmanly to say they cannot do it. This letter is in no sense an order.

Yours, truly,
A Lincoln"

Lincoln could undoubtedly have benefited from the decisiveness of a charismatic general such as Thomas "Stonewall" Jackson, one of the great heroes of the Civil War. A career soldier who had been a professor at the Virginia Military Institute in the years before the conflict, Jackson was austere, godly, and faintly eccentric. He was revered by his soldiers and trusted implicitly by his military superiors.

He did not appreciate politicians' meddling, however, and early in 1862 threatened to resign after Judah Benjamin, the Confederate Secretary for War, questioned his movements in relation to reinforcing Loring's troops in the Shenandoah Valley. "With such interference in my command I cannot expect to be of much service in the field…I respectfully request that the President will accept my resignation from the army." He recounts the incident in a letter to his friend, Rev. (Dr.) Francis McFarland of Augusta County, Virginia.

"Winchester
Feby 11th 1862

My dear Doctor

Your very kind and Christian letter respecting my proposed withdrawal from Field Service has been received, and be assured that it met with a cordial reception. My desire to serve our cause is undiminished, but I am in active service not because it is more congenial to my taste, but from a sense of duty. The moment that my services are not required in the field I desire to return to the Institute.

After God had restored to us the county of Morgan East of the Big Capon River and the most valuable portion of Hampshire County, and was still driving the enemy from this Military District, the Secretary of War without consulting me upon the subject, sent an order to me stating that he has information, that Genl. Loring's command is in danger of being cut off, and directs me to order him back to Winchester immediately, thus unnecessarily abandoning to the enemy what had been restored to us. If such a policy as that was to be pursued by the Secretary at his desk far removed from the theatre of war, ruin must result to our cause, and I feel called upon to utter my strongest protest against such a ruinous policy, and this I designed doing by offering to resign, rather than be the willful instrument of carrying out a ruinous policy. So far as the secretary may have shown indignity to me personally, that is not a matter to be considered in times like the present. I am satisfied that my course was a good one for our cause, the effect that it may injuriously have in the estimation of men respecting me, is of but little moment. I say it humbly but with the hope that you will live to see that my course has been what it should have been. I am every ready to remain in the field when I can have a prospect of being useful there. Pray that I may be useful.

I am sincerely your friend
T.J. Jackson"

When Jackson was killed a year later, a victim of "friendly" fire at the Battle of Chancellorsville, he was widely mourned. Lee wondered how he would replace him, and even his enemies admitted he was "the bravest of the brave." Private Henry Dedrick of the 52nd Virginia Infantry wrote to his father-in-law to report on the battle, the loss of Jackson, and to complain about the paucity of supplies.

"Spotsylvania Co. Virginia. Camp near Hamilton's Crossing. May 10th 1863

Dear Father—
I take this opportunity to drop you a few to answer your few lines that I received from you this evening. I was glad to hear from you all and to hear that you are well. I am well at present and hope when these few lines comes to hand they may find you all enjoying the same blessing of god a resting upon you.

You said that you heard that Gen. Jackson had a fight. It was not only him it was all of the troops. We had one of the hardest fights that we ever had since the war begun. General Jackson has lost one of his arms and [has] now got the pneumonia. He is not expected to live. He was shot by our own pickets. He got out side of our pickets after night and he come up in a gallop and they fired on him and wounded him and all of his guard but one. Our loss is said to be twenty thousand killed wounded and missing. I don't know what the [loss] of the enemy was but it must be terrible. I have just heard that General Jackson was dead. If he is it is a great loss to the Southern confederacy...

If we stay here I wish you would come down and bring me something to eat for we don't get half enough and I can't stand it. If you do come you can bring something along and make more off of it [than] you can make any other way. You can get from 50 to 75 cents for a pie, and tobacco is very high. You can sell most anything atall, potatoes 50 cents per quart. Thread is very high and I have two overcoats and a good blanket I would like to send home. If I had them at home I wouldn't take less than 60 dollars for them. If you come and if we are at the same place you can come to Hamilton's Crossing, that is [with]in two miles of our camp.

Joshua Robison [Robinson?] and Adam Pannell sends their best respects to you all. I must close for this time. You will please excuse me for this. May god bless you all. Write soon.
H. H. Dedrick to Elijah Balsley."

Above: Company A, 9th Indiana Infantry saw extensive service in Tennessee, Georgia, and South Carolina.

After Chancellorsville, Lee, having had victory snatched from him so many times, was determined to achieve a decisive win for the Confederacy. He invaded the North and attacked the forces of the Union in Pennsylvania, at Gettysburg, a three-day-long battle which ended in failure for the South. It was the largest battle of the Civil War and, along with Vicksburg, proved to be a turning point. After it, the Confederacy never really came close to threatening Northern dominance again. Lee lost about a third of his army, yet was determined to withdraw with the remainder and remained calm and implacable in the face of further Union pursuit under Meade. A few days later he wrote to his wife:

"The consequences of war are horrid enough at best, surrounded by all the ameliorations of civilisation and Christianity. I am very sorry for the injuries done the family at Hickory Hill, and particularly that our dear old Uncle Williams, in his eightieth year, should be subjected to such treatment. But we cannot help it, and must endure it.

You will, however, learn before this reaches you that our success at Gettysburg was not so great as reported—in fact, that we failed to drive the enemy from his position, and that our army withdrew to the Potomac. Had the river not unexpectedly risen, all would have been well with us; but God, in His all-wise providence, willed otherwise, and our communications have been interrupted and almost cut off.

The waters have subsided to about four feet, and, if they continue, by to-morrow, I hope, our communications will be open. I trust that a merciful God, our only hope and refuge, will not desert us in this hour of need, and will deliver us by His almighty hand, that the whole world may recognise His power and all hearts be lifted up in adoration and praise of His unbounded loving-kindness. We must, however, submit to His almighty will, whatever that may be.
"May God guide and protect us all is my constant prayer."

Many letters touch on the deprivations of the Confederate troops. The Confederacy was permanently short of cash and its soldiers suffered accordingly. By the time of the Battle of Shiloh in 1862, it is estimated that over 60 percent of the men had to wear looted Union uniforms, increasing the chances of accidents arising from mistaken identity. Shoes were a particular problem, and the hackneyed image of "barefoot Johnny Reb" has a sound basis in fact. Both sides had to march immense distances over terrain that quickly ruined footwear, but the Confederates had particular trouble obtaining new stores, and soldiers were often excluded from the battlefield for lack of shoes. Lee wrote many times to the Confederate Quartermaster urging him to procure more supplies. In the cold winter of January 1864, supplies were particularly sparse:

"General,
The want of shoes and blankets in this army continues to cause much suffering and to impair its efficiency. In one regiment I am informed that there are only fifty men with serviceable shoes, and a brigade that recently went on picket was compelled to leave several hundred men in camp, who were unable to bear the exposure of duty, being destitute of shoes and blankets... The supply, by running the blockade, has become so precarious that I think we should turn our attention chiefly to our own resources, and I should like to be informed how far the latter can be counted upon... I trust that no efforts will be spared to develop our own resources of supply, as a further dependence upon those from abroad can result in nothing but increase of suffering and want.

I am, with great respect, Your obedient servant,

R. E. Lee, General."

The supply of Confederate rations was also uncertain, hampered by transportation difficulties as well as a universal shortage of food in the Southern states. Soldiers on both sides foraged to improve their diets and hoped that their families would send them food to liven up their diets. Lt. Col. William Bentley of the 24th Virginian Infantry remarked in a letter to his mother in June 1862:

"Provisions are very scarce and very indifferent. I get a little coffee by paying two dollars a pound & sixty five cents a pound for bacon. I fared well (after I got so that I could eat something) at Mr. Robertson's. I never drank better coffee anywhere. Mr. Christian advised me to not even offer him pay—that it might offend him. He made me promise to come back if I got sick again & said I must come to see him whenever I could get out of camp."

This letter from Giles S. Thomas, serving in the Union Army of the Mississippi, recounts his part in the siege of Vicksburg. He also mentions passing through a plantation belonging to the Confederate president's family, and, by the sound of things, looting it.

"Mississippi Two miles from Jackson.
July 16th 1863

My dear Parrents,
I have the opportunity of sending a letter [by] to Indianapolis by the drafted men they will leave in a day or two and it being the only chance to send a letter I thought I would try and write a few lines to let you know how we are getting a long My dear friends I am truly glad that I still have the pleasure of telling [you] that we are in good health and enjoying our selves the best we can [in the place] under the present circumstance that we are in at the present time. I have not time to write this evening so I will write a few lines.

We Marched to this place We had some very hard Marching and water very poor and Scarce the heat was very hard on the men we advanced with in 1 mile of Jackson and there we stopped and have been Skirmishing for the last four days yesterday evening was relieved and fell back for rest We lost 1 man and 1 wounded in the head. My position in ranks is Color Guard it is rather a dangerous place but a very honorable place. We have not received a letter from home for over [2] weeks I received 1 from Aunt Martha a few day a go Mailed the 30th June. The 46th Regt is on our right a bout 3 miles from here I heard Jonas Stiver was dead Oh how I would like to See uncle George but we have no chance to See him the road that goes from here to the landing goes pass where the 46th was in a fight when we came through we did not come in the road half the time and did not see the place I think the place is called Champion Hill One of our men that was with the wagon train said they saw the place and where the 46th men was buried

Well I have learnt how it goes to have the balls pass by I have had some [pass] cut pretty close but not hurt yet I have not got [use?] to these big balls and think I will not they are not very pleasant I assure you but we have to put up with them the best we can We are on the West Side of Jackson in the front Since we came here we have had some pretty Sharp living We had for 4 days but water and crackers but since we was relieved we have recruited up a gain we have plenty of corn and peaches to all distraction but the peaches is not quite ripe When we come to this place we passed through Jeff Davis Brothers plantat[ion] and close to Old Jeffs farm Col. Dehart got a very nice Cane with Jeffs nam engraved on the cane very nice it was found in Jeffs house or his brothers. The Col. Carys it with him all the time he is very proud of his present

I could write you a long letter but I must Stop

Our things is left back to the landing and my paper is all their the men have not had a change of clothes for over 3 weeks and you can Judge how we all look by this time Marching in the dust where it is Sho[e mou]th d[e]ep. Father George and I sent $35.00 home with the Chaplain but I think you will get it before you get this letter the Chap. sent it from Laf. or India. by Express. No more at the present I send you all my love and best respects.

Giles S. Thomas.
Direct letters 99th Regt Ind Vol. Army of the Miss."

Above: Federal cavalry engage Confederate troops at Yellow Tavern, near Richmond, Virginia, on May 11, 1864.

Over half a million soldiers became prisoners of war at some time during the conflict, and about half of that number were released on condition that they agreed not to bear arms again. Napoleon B. Brisbane, a surgeon serving with the 2nd Ohio Cavalry regiment, was unlucky on several counts. He was not only captured twice, but as a doctor he was especially vulnerable: tied down by caring for patients, he could not, in all conscience, try to escape. His letters show that he was resigned to his fate and in this one, he describes the recapture of Winchester by Union forces, along with the resulting Confederate retreat.

"Winchester, Virginia
September 24, 1864
Dear Brother and Sister—
I sat down two or three days ago to write this to you but some circumstance occurred to stop me and I did not write. But will finish it today and send it post haste.

I was a prisoner five weeks to the day our troops recaptured me at this place, and during the time had no chance of letting you know of my whereabouts. So you see I was not to blame this time. I wrote one letter to you and sent by a citizen who said he would get it through for me.

Last Monday morning I was awakened by the heavy booming of artillery and upon inquiring the case, was informed that the Yanks were only about two or three miles from town and had made a demonstration at day light. I judged by the time and the length of the firing that we were to have a general engagement that day and oh, how I prayed for success to our arms, for I knew what a formidable antagonist they would have to cope with, and well I knew that day would bring the hardest fighting ever done in the valley. All day the cannon bellowed and once in a while a breeze would bring the faint report of firearms, rifles, muskets, and carbines. But along in the afternoon, the small arms became quite plain and at length cheers could be heard, and a shell would come over me from the Yankee Battery.

Then commenced one of the greatest panic retreats I ever saw without any exception, and the horses, mules & men all went along with their tails up (excuse the last remark, the latter's tails were down). The old 8th Corps done wonders in that day and redeemed itself from all other stains. While the rebels were retreating through town a shell from one of our Batteries came through our Hospital, going over two beds and striking the third one smashing it to splinters, tearing the straw out of the mattress and disappeared through the other side of the house, not hurting a man. The bed was occupied by a man with a fractured thigh but was not hurt. Sheridan is a trump, and is just whipping them as they go.

I am not on duty at present. Have been sick but am now quite well again. We had about thirty five hundred wounded here including Rebs. We captured nearly all their wounded. I stayed on duty as long as I could but had to give up. Was sick when the fight came off. Would like to go home but no chance, every thing is busy. Captured about four thousand seven hundred prisoners here, and since captured some seventeen hundred. About eleven hundred dead on the field of both sides. Up to this time have taken thirty one pieces of artillery with numbers of wagons & horse. Cannot tell how long will stay here. Write soon to your brother. N. B. Brisbine."

In 1864, General U.S. Grant assumed command of the whole Union army and entrusted Sherman with the task of destroying J. E. Johnstons' Army of Tennessee. In his report of operations, Grant noted, "General Sherman was instructed to move against Johnston's army, to break it up, and to go into the interior of the enemy's country as far as he could, inflicting all the damage he could upon their war resources." This maneuver has become infamous as Sherman's "March to the Sea" from Tennessee to Georgia, and marked a new departure in military tactics; the brutal policy of destroying everything in the Union army's path was a deliberate attempt to demoralize civilians and annihilate the economic infrastructure of the South. William Tecumseh Sherman, a man named for a First Nation warrior, and who subsequently had one of World War II's toughest tanks named after him, was, rather fittingly, the instigator of "total war." Sherman's letters and dispatches prove that here was another general with an effective and immediate style of communication.

Right: A man of courage, conviction, and strategic genius, Ulysses S. Grant (1822–1885), was one of the outstanding commanders of the Civil War. Genuinely troubled by the division of the Union, Grant arranged generous surrender terms for the Confederates at war's end, announcing "The war is over. The Rebels are our countrymen again."

"Kingston, GA., October 11, 1864—11 a.m.

Lieutenant-General Grant:

Hood moved his army from Palmetto Station across by Dallas and Cedartown, and is now on the Coosa River, south of Rome. He threw one corps on my road at Acworth, and I was forced to follow. I hold Atlanta with the Twentieth Corps, and have strong detachments along my line. This reduces my active force to a comparatively small army. We cannot remain here on the defensive. With the 25,000 men, and the bold cavalry he has, he can constantly break my roads. I would infinitely prefer to make a wreck of the road and of the country from Chattanooga to Atlanta, including the latter city, send back all my wounded and worthless, and, with my effective army, move through Georgia, smashing things to the sea. Hood may turn into Tennessee and Kentucky, but I believe he will be forced to follow me. Instead of my being on the defensive, I would be on the offensive; instead of guessing at what he means to do, he would have to guess at my plans. The difference in war is full 25 per cent. I can make Savannah, Charleston, or the mouth of the Chattahoochee. Answer quick, as I know we will not have the telegraph long.

W. T. Sherman,
Major-General."

In early September, Sherman had beaten off Hood and occupied Atlanta, much to the consternation of the local people who had seen the havoc wreaked across the South at first hand. Sherman was intent on razing the city to the ground, but first ordered the evacuation of the citizens. The exchange of letters between the mayor and the general illustrate the harsh realities of the situation for the innocent civilians.

Left: William T. Sherman (1820–1891) was an aggressive general possessed of exceptional military skill, although in 1861–1862 he had suffered from emotional problems and depression. By 1864, however, he executed a stunning logistical achievement in leading an army of 62,000 men across Georgia, vowing to cripple the enemy's military resources. "I can make Georgia howl," he promised.

"Atlanta, Georgia, September 11, 1864.
Major-General W. T. Sherman.

Sir: We the undersigned, Mayor and two of the Council for the city of Atlanta, for the time being the only legal organ of the people of the said city, to express their wants and wishes, ask leave most earnestly but respectfully to petition you to reconsider the order requiring them to leave Atlanta

At first view, it struck us that the measure would involve extraordinary hardship and loss, but since we have seen the practical execution of it so far as it has progressed, and the individual condition of the people, and heard their statements as to the inconveniences, loss, and suffering attending it, we are satisfied that the amount of it will involve in the aggregate consequences appalling and heart-rending.

Many poor women are in advanced state of pregnancy, others now having young children, and whose husbands for the greater part are either in the army, prisoners, or dead. Some say: "I have such a one sick at my house; who will wait on them when I am gone?" Others say: "What are we to do? We have no house to go to, and no means to buy, build, or rent any; no parents, relatives, or friends, to go to." Another says: "I will try and take this or that article of property, but such and such things I must leave behind, though I need them much." We reply to them: "General Sherman will carry your property to Rough and Ready, and General Hood will take it thence on." And they will reply that: "But I want to leave the railroad at such a place, and cannot get conveyance from there on."

We only refer to a few facts, to try to illustrate in part how this measure will operate in practice. As you advanced, the people north of this fell back; and before your arrival here, a large portion of the people had retired south, so that the country south of this is already crowded, and without houses enough to accommodate the people, and we are informed that many are now staying in churches and other out-buildings.

This being so, how is it possible for the people still here (mostly women and children) to find any shelter? And how can they live through the winter in the woods—no shelter or subsistence, in the midst of strangers who know them not, and without the power to assist them much, if they were willing to do so?

This is but a feeble picture of the consequences of this measure. You know the woe, the horrors, and the suffering, cannot be described by words; imagination can only conceive of it, and we ask you to take these things into consideration.

We know your mind and time are constantly occupied with the duties of your command, which almost deters us from asking your attention to this matter, but thought it might be that you had not considered this subject in all of its awful consequences, and that on more reflection you, we hope, would not make this people an exception to all mankind, for we know that no such instance ever having occurred—surely never in the United States—and what has this helpless people done, that they should be driven from their homes, to wander strangers and outcasts, and exiles, and to subsist on charity?

We do not know as yet the number of people still here; of those who are here, we are satisfied a respectable number, if allowed to remain at home, could subsist for several months without assistance, and a respectable number for a much longer time, and who might not need assistance at any time.

In conclusion, we most earnestly and solemnly petition you to reconsider this order, or modify it, and suffer this unfortunate people to remain at home, and enjoy what little means they have.

Respectfully submitted:

James M. Calhoun, Mayor
E.E. Rawson, Councilman.
S.C. Wells, Councilman."

Sherman's reply was reasoned and attempted to explain his actions in the most utilitarian terms. He was working on a theory of the greatest good for the greatest number, and by his logic, the people of Atlanta had to suffer in order to force the surrender of the Confederacy. He left the mayor in no doubt as to his intentions, bleakly stating, "You might as well appeal against the thunder-storm as against these terrible hardships of war." His letter justifies his actions under the rules of engagement and sets out exactly why he believes he is right to wage war on the south in the interests of the Union.

Right: A selection of Union correspondence including: an appointment document issued by the 19th Ohio Volunteers; a letter from a prisoner in Danville, Virginia; a soldier's letter; a pass issued by Provost Marshall, July 14, 1861; and letters featuring patriotic vignettes.

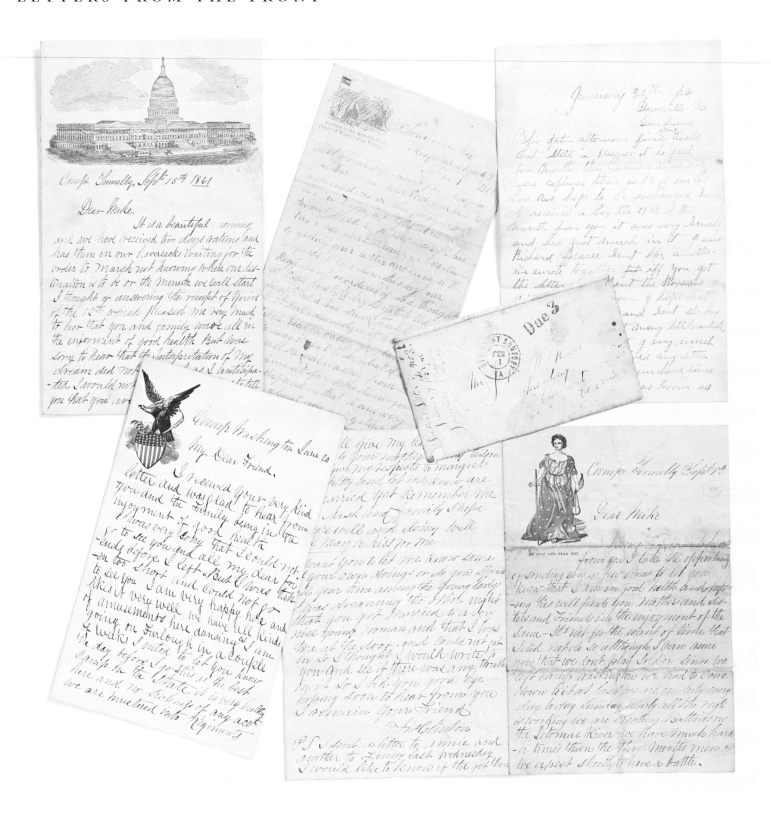

"Headquarters Military Division of the Mississippi,
in the Field, Atlanta, Georgia, September 12, 1864.

James M. Calhoun, Mayor, E.E. Rawson, S.C. Wells, representing
City Council of Atlanta.

Gentlemen: I have your letter of the 11th, in the nature of a petition to revoke my orders removing all the inhabitants from Atlanta. I have read it carefully, and give full credit to your statements of the distress that will be occasioned, any yet shall not revoke my orders, because they were not designed to meet the humanities of the case, but to prepare for the future struggles in which millions of good people outside of Atlanta have a deep interest. We must have peace, not only in Atlanta, but in all America. To secure this, we must stop the war that now desolates our once happy and favored country. To stop war, we must defeat the rebel armies which are now arrayed against the laws and Constitution that all must respect and obey. To defeat those armies, we must prepare the way to reach them in their recesses, provided with the arms and instruments which enable us to accomplish our purpose. Now I know the vindictive nature of our enemy, that we may have many years of military operations from this quarter; and, therefore, deem it wise and prudent to prepare in time. The use of Atlanta for warlike purposes is inconsistent with its character as a home for families. There will be no manufactures, commerce, or agriculture here, for the maintenance of families, and sooner or later want will compel the inhabitants to go. Why not go now, when all the arrangements are completed for the transfer, instead of waiting till the plunging shot of contending armies will renew the scenes of the past month? Of course, I do not apprehend any such thing at this moment, but you do not suppose this army will be here until the war is over. I cannot discuss this subject with you fairly, because I cannot impart to you what we propose to do, but I assert that our military plans make it necessary for the inhabitants to go away, and I can only renew my offer of services to make their exodus in any direction as easy and comfortable as possible.

You cannot qualify war in harsher terms than I will. War is cruelty, and you cannot refine it; and those who brought war into our country deserve all the curses and maledictions a people can pour out. I know I had no hand in making this war, and I know I will make more sacrifices to-day than any of you to secure peace. But you cannot have peace and a division of our country. If the United States submits to a division now, it will not stop, but will go on until we reap the fate of Mexico, which is eternal war. The United States does and must assert its authority, wherever it once had power; for, if it relaxes one bit to pressure, it is gone, and I believe that such is the national feeling. This feeling assumes various shapes, but always comes back to that of Union. Once admit the Union, once more acknowledge the authority of the national Government, and, instead of devoting your houses and streets and roads to the dread uses of war, I and this army become at once your protectors and supporters, shielding you from danger, let it come from what quarter it may. I know that a few individuals cannot resist a torrent of error and passion, such as swept the South into rebellion, but you can point out, so that we may know those who desire a government, and those who insist on war and its desolation.

You might as well appeal against the thunder-storm as against these terrible hardships of war. They are inevitable, and the only way the people of Atlanta can hope once more to live in peace and quiet at home, is to stop the war, which can only be done by admitting that it began in error and is perpetuated in pride.

We don't want your negroes, or your horses, or your houses, or your hands, or any thing that you have, but we do want and will have a just obedience to the laws of the United States. That we will have, and, if it involves the destruction of your improvements, we cannot help it.

You have heretofore read public sentiment in your newspapers, that live by falsehood and excitement; and the quicker you seek for truth in other quarters, the better. I repeat then that, by the original compact of Government, the United States had certain rights in Georgia, which have never been relinquished and never will be; that the South began war by seizing forts, arsenals, mints, custom-houses, etc., etc., long before Mr. Lincoln was installed, and before the South had one jot or title of provocation. I myself have seen in Missouri, Kentucky, Tennessee, and Mississippi, hundreds of thousands of women and children fleeing from your armies and desperadoes, hungry and with bleeding feet. In Memphis, Vicksburg, and Mississippi, we fed thousands upon thousands of families of rebel soldiers left in our hands, and whom we could not see starve. Now that war comes home to you, you feel very different. You depreciate its horrors, but did not feel them when you sent car-loads of soldiers and ammunition, and moulded shells and shot, to carry war into Kentucky and Tennessee, to desolate the homes of hundreds of thousands of good people who only asked to live in peace at their old homes, and under the Government of their inheritance. But these comparisons are idle. I want peace, and believe it can only be reached through union and war, and I will ever conduct war with a view to perfect and early success.

But, my dear sirs, when peace does come, you may call on me for any thing. Then I will share with you the last cracker, and watch with you to shield your homes and families against danger from every quarter.

Now you must go, and take with you the old and feeble, feed and nurse them, and build for them, in more quiet places, proper habitations to shield them against the weather until the mad passions of men cool down, and allow the Union and peace once more to settle over your old homes at Atlanta. Yours in haste,

W.T. Sherman, Major-General commanding."

If, in 1861, the President could dismiss the impending war as an "insurrection," by 1865, he was under no illusion about the impact of his actions. It is a truism that in war, old men send young men to their deaths, and it is clear from this letter that Lincoln bore these responsibilities heavily.

"Executive Mansion,
Washington,
November 21, 1864.

Mrs. Bixby,
Boston, Massachusetts:

Dear Madam,

I have been shown in the files of the War Department a statement of the Adjutant-General of Massachusetts that you are the mother of

five sons who have died gloriously on the field of battle. I feel how weak and fruitless must be any words of mine which should attempt to beguile you from the grief of a loss so overwhelming. But I cannot refrain from tendering to you the consolation that may be found in the thanks of the Republic they died to save. I pray that our Heavenly Father may assuage the anguish of your bereavement, and leave you only the cherished memory of the loved and lost, and the solemn pride that must be yours to have laid so costly a sacrifice upon the altar of freedom.

Yours very sincerely and respectfully,

Abraham Lincoln."

Right: Pickets trading between the lines.

Right: A regimental Christmas card sent by soldiers during World War I.

Far right: The first Allied offensive of the Battle of the Somme in 1916 failed to break through German lines prolonging the costly trench warfare of World War I.

World War I 1914–1918

Few wars simply erupt out of nowhere—they are usually preceded by years of resentment festering between the combatant nations. This is particularly true of World War I, but in this case the rancor and bitterness were deep-seated and were shared between several ethnic groups and countries. War had long been expected, as German aggrandizement in the early years of the 20th century threatened the status quo of Europe and the British Empire, and the Austro-Hungarian empire based its survival on the destruction of Balkan nationalism. That the murder of a Hapsburg prince in Sarajevo in 1914 could precipitate four years of bloodletting and draw in Britain, France, Russia, and eventually the U.S.A. seemed incredible to many, but it provided an excuse for years of barely suppressed hostility.

As men cheerfully rushed to join up in August 1914, answering Kitchener's call for 100,000 men, they assured each other that "it would all be over by Christmas." Tragically, they were wrong, and they were not to enjoy a peaceful Christmas until 1918, by which time, over nine million men had been slaughtered.

The casualty figures are horrific and become even more so when broken down; 300 a day at Ypres in 1915; 60,000 casualties (19,000 dead) on the morning of July 1, 1916, the first day of the Battle of the Somme; almost half a million at Passchendaele in 1917. The immaculate war graves that dot northern France or the simple war memorials in hundreds of towns and villages remain as memorials to the millions of named dead. Then the number of names on the Menin Gate in Ypres are to be considered: 54,000 soldiers with no known grave, their remains lost in the mud of Flanders.

The letters of combatants living through quite extraordinary, often inhuman sights and sounds remain fascinating and often poignant. That men from sophisticated industrialized societies could accept living in the primitive subterranean, muddy conditions of the trenches of Flanders, with rats and often corpses for company seems inconceivable now. Their letters home certainly do not gloss over the facts of their discomfort and many are peppered with requests for warm clothing, blankets, gloves, and hats to

Above: A tourist inspects sandbags in a World War I trench, in 1919.

augment their regulation equipment. Most writers, however, were constrained not only by the official censor who eliminated information deemed valuable to the enemy, but also by their feelings for their correspondents. Men knew that mothers, wives, and sweethearts would be worried by their participation in battle and tried not to dwell on the true misery and danger of their existence. Many suppressed their feelings and some emerged from the trenches with shell shock and mental problems that haunted them for the rest of their lives.

Most letters home were censored, although there were some exemptions. In the British army field postcards remained uncensored and urgent letters were enclosed in the "green envelope." The writers had to sign a printed note on the back of this envelope stating : "I certify on my honor that the contents of this envelope refer to nothing but private and family matters."

Leslie Green joined the Territorial Army in 1912–1913 aged 17 or 18, one of many thousands of men who were part-time, "weekend" soldiers. His unit, the Retford Company, 8th Battalion Sherwood Foresters, Notts and Derby Regiment, was mobilized as soon as war broke out in 1914, and after three months' intensive training, he was sent to France in 1915. A brave and sensitive man, Leslie Green understood how his family would react on hearing that he had volunteered for active service, but he was a patriotic young man and a committed Christian, and firmly believed that it was his duty to go to war. This letter was written a week after war was declared:

"Aug 12th 1914

Dear Dad,

...this morning the battalion paraded in Clarence Road School grounds to be addressed by the Brigadier General. He explained quite briefly the seriousness of the war at present, also the necessity of every man in the Batt to volunteer for active service. He was so very disappointed with the answers to the questions [over whether men would volunteer immediately for service in theatres of active operations]... Things are quite more serious with England than is generally imagined.

He asked all the captains of companies to go round each coy and get to know the percentage of volunteers. There was about 5% of our coy including myself. After this had been done the colonel asked the batt to do their duty and he hoped no man would refuse. He said that every man must consider the welfare of the empire first and that wives, children, sweethearts and business must go to the wall. He pointed out that he as well as all the other officers were having to leave their families and businesses. Nest, all NCOs were called to a meeting at which we decided to follow the colonel into active service or anywhere on earth. I was talking to Lt James afterwards and he told me that it could not have come at a worse time with him. He told me that if we should go he would get married and then go in for it all he was worth...

The colonel told us the plan of campaign as far as he knew was that Lord Kitchener is massing a great army to take Berlin...

Please be careful how you break the news to mother..."

[From *Lest we Forget* by John W. Green. Privately published letter from his father Sgt. W. L. Green, Retford Co (TA), 8th Bn Sherwood Foresters, Notts & Derby Regt.]

The initial Von Schlieffen plan was for the Germans to sweep through Belgium, Luxembourg, and northern France, enveloping Paris and defeating the French in under six weeks. The German High Command did not seriously believe that Britain would uphold their promise to protect Belgian neutrality; the rulers of Germany and Great Britain were cousins, and war between the two nations was surely unlikely. However, Britain declared war and immediately sent the British Expeditionary Force (BEF) to defend Belgium. By Christmas 1914, both sides had dug in. Trenches snaked across northern France and Belgium, forming a continuous frontier from the North Sea to Switzerland. With nearly three quarters of a million men mobilized, the British supply lines became clogged with mail at Christmas: a quarter of a million parcels were sent to Flanders before the last Christmas posting date, along with 2.5 million letters.

The situation around Ypres had reached something of a stalemate in the spring of 1915, although sniping was continuous, and in April the Germans unleashed a new weapon: chlorine gas, which floated over the battlefield with deadly effect. Lieutenant Corporal Cecil East was 23, a volunteer with the Honourable Artillery Company, a Territorial unit which recruited most of its troops from the City of London. He provides an excellent insight into life in the trenches and in the build up to Second Ypres seems resolutely cheerful, partly in the face of happy news from home. He was able to celebrate the birth of his niece with champagne. He seems to have spent a lot of time drinking and gambling, which in view of his untimely death a month later, seems perfectly apposite for a young man of 23. His letter illustrates the comparative speed with which mail traveled between England and the front. Cecil is replying to a card sent to him on April 4 at the earliest, and used a "green envelope" to ensure that his letter was sent quickly.

"9 April 1915

My dear Dorothy and Dudley,
I was very glad to get your pc [postcard] (which I received while in a very wet reserve trench) saying that the kid had faced the tapes alright and that D and the aforesaid kid were fit and well. I notice you put no date on the card. Surely it was not April 1?

Things in the Marriage, Birth and Death line seem brisk in our family at the moment—let's hope I don't help mess things with the last, as the first two are unfortunately (or fortunately) denied me.

Well the idea of this letter was to congratulate you (or sympathise, with, I'm damned if I know which) both on the happy event and to wish Dorothy and the infant the best of luck. I was tickled to death when I heard it was a she-child and imagined the curses heaped upon the poor thing. Still it's a little more off the income tax and will save the trouble of wondering in time to come 'what to do with our boys'.

We have had a very strenuous time lately and shall have the first full night's rest tonight for nearly three weeks. Still we have had some fun and have had a lot of fun lately as there have been so many things to celebrate (Births etc, etc.) the lads were very glad to have something else to drink to and we had done the family wedding and the engagement and had even done Bismarck's birthday (I hope this wasn't treason). We have found some most excellent stiff Moet at 10.50 which goes down with a click at about 11 o'clock in the morning. I have tried some dozens of different makes out here from 5 francs upwards, but this is the finest drink I have ever had. We did the war baby this morning in it. If you know of anything else for us to wet first let me know.

Money has been plentiful up to now, mostly owing poker, but at the moment I am frantically calling up loans and hope to receive a big one tomorrow. We play a lot of poker. We played for two days in the trench this last time and had 60 francs from a man in another section, although I did not win [illegible] personally this time, but we never mind as long as we have the money in the section...

We came down after four days in the open and had a grand time, although wet and muddy again and sniped at a good deal. Suppose we shall do fatigues up to the trenches most nights while we are here. The longer we stay out the harder we have to work. I shall try for commission in RN [illegible] but it is a devil of a job to get a Com [mission] that's the rub.

Well I am turning on my soft couch now. We thank God for a full night's sleep on dry boards these days (or rather nights). What a life! I often laugh and wonder what it all really means. It has been beaten to a frazzle. I am always glad to get your letters.

Cheerioh

Cecil"

By 1916, Leslie Green was a sergeant and having survived the Ypres Salient of 1915, he won the Military Medal in October of the same year for his actions at the Hohenzollern Redoubt between Lens and Bethune, an experience he described as "hell with the lid off." "I was given the strength and preserved alive in face of what appeared to be certain death," he wrote to his parents. Sergeant Green's battalion fought around Vimy in early 1916, dealing with German mining activity. It was arduous, nerve-jangling work

Above: British troops march towards trenches near Ypres at the Western Front.

and in June 1916, Sergeant Green was tired and a little depressed by the relentless fighting. After nearly two years of fighting, he was battle-hardened and far more experienced than the troops of "Kitchener's Army," the men who enlisted during the great recruiting drive of 1914–1915 and were, by 1916, trained and being sent to units in France.

"Rest Billets, France
28/6/16

Dear Dad, Mother and All,

...We came out of the Foucqueviller trenches late last night very fatigued after spending eight days there in the most awful conditions I have ever experienced. I suppose the trenches at Veil-Chappel which I missed whilst acting CQMS [Company Quartermaster Sergeant] were similar.

The trenches in question were very badly constructed and minus dugouts for shelter. In the course of last week's weather we had wind, rain, frost and snow which added to the joys of trench life. As usual we were not destined to get off scot free, we had several casualties, the enemy were fairly quiet but windy. One night they blew up a mine just on the right of our trench and occupied the crater which was retaken by the 5th Batt. With a good few casualties. Well, Dad and Mum I will not detail any more troubles, we all have to put up with them. There is just one thing which upset my apple cart more than anything, I haven't the confidence in our present compliment of officers and a great majority of the men who are inexperienced and windy. No doubt the bearer of this letter, A Parsons will tell you a little bit about things.

By jove it was a treat to get down to kip last night after eight days with wet feet and legs. You know whilst in the trenches we never have our equipment off. We took over these trenches from the French just over three weeks ago...

Well we are back again at rest billets and making the most of our rest. I am earnestly looking forward to the end of this war, at times it gets one's nerves. I feel quite an old soldier now-a-days. I have handed over the SMs [sergeant major's] job now to the original one, it was very instructive... I am in the pink of condition considering, just fagged out with the additional strain owing to rotten weather..."

Lieutenant John Staniforth of the 7th Leinsters, who wrote the next letter, had spent a year in barracks in Fermoy, County Cork, Ireland. He wrote many amusing letters to his family and was delighted when the regiment was finally ordered to England for more intensive training. His account of the actual logistics of troop movement during wartime tells a familiar story of muddle mixed with strict military drill. He makes interesting comments about keeping the soldiers "locked in:" this officer was in charge of draftees, rather than volunteers, and he mentions that two managed to escape. The contrast between the officers' lifestyle and that of the other ranks is quite striking. The enlisted men marched from the camp to the station while the officers went in a car; other ranks emerged disheveled from their overnight journey from Dublin and were rewarded with breakfast and a packet of cigarettes, while the officers had time for a leisurely bath at a local hotel and a sumptuous breakfast.

"Kilworth Camp,
Fermoy.
22.8.1915

My Dear Ones,

We have our official notice to quit now—at least, we have our destination, though not the date. The whole of this Division is to go to Larkhill, which is somewhere in the middle of Salisbury Plain, though I can't find it on the map...

Later (7 September 1915): I've unpacked this again, at the other end of our journey, since when I've received two of your letters, but no telegram. I could not telegraph to you our date of crossing or any other particulars, as you asked. As a matter of fact I was in charge of the postal arrangements myself (signalling officer again), with express instructions to censor just that kind of telegram, along with any other information, however general, of our movements; so it would not have looked well to have set the example myself...

We paraded the whole crowd left in the camp, and found we were richer by this time by two new recruits come to join their regiment, five men recalled from furlough too late to go with the battalion, and three Royal Irishmen who had missed their crowd when it went out the day before. We gave them each sixpence as travelling allowance, and started them off down the road under an N.C.O. Then we

---

finished packing our own kit, telephoned for a motor, paid one last visit to all the barrack-rooms and camp buildings, and went to get a "biting-on" at our old friend the Soldiers Home.

When the car came we whizzed down to Fermoy, arriving of course before the men, and arranged with the station-master about carriages, and also got the 40-odd portions of bread from the baker ready for distributing. We went to the Fermoy Soldiers Home as well and arranged one last meal for them at 3d a head. By the time we had this done they were just arriving, so we paraded them on the platform, counted heads, stacked their gear and mounted a baggage-guard over it, and packed them off to eat their last Irish meal.

Twenty minutes before train-time we fished them back, told them off to their compartments, and got them entrained, each man with all his kit, eight to a carriage, and turned the key on them. We wired to Mallow that we had a detachment for the Dublin mail, and instructed them to have extra coaches in readiness there; we wired to the Railway Transport Officer at Kingstown to arrange for embarkation on the steamer; we wired to the battalion at Aldershot to notify them of our intended departure (telegrams are cheap On His Majesty's Service), and despatched a written message to Divisional headquarters stating that all instructions as to handing-over had been carried out and giving particulars of the steps we had taken to consign things left behind and instructions as to their disposal.

Then at last we took our seats in the train, feeling we had done all things man could do (even to the buying a sufficiency of cigarettes)—and found we hadn't a match between us... At Kingstown we had our only mishap. The men of course were locked in; but while the N.C.O. in charge of one compartment was leaning out talking to a porter on the platform, two of them did a dive out of the other window, which was open, and cut stick for the town (both Dublin men, of course), and we haven't seen them since. They'll be brought back in a few days, no doubt, but all the same it was a pity. Otherwise we lost no more from the draft all the way across...

[On arrival in London] I led them down into the tube station (we went down in two lifts, and I just managed to herd back the other half from rushing away to a train for Shepherds Bush or the Elephant & Castle or somewhere at the back of God's world) and explained to them that the trains here are not exactly the kind of easy-going Irish affairs they had been used to, which would wait half-an-hour for them to get leisurely on board. Apparently they took this to heart, for when the train pulled in there was a stampede and they nipped in for their lives like a lot of bunnies going to earth when a man comes round the corner with a gun. In a couple of seconds there wasn't a trace of them to be seen. They made themselves awful unpopular with their stampede, too, because the train was very crowded with folk going to work, and these 50 men who surged in all stuck out a couple of feet all round with their rifles and tins and blankets and kitbags.

At Waterloo we saw their breakfast, and gave them a packet of Woodbines each; and then, as we couldn't get a train down till 10.30, we turned them loose on the platform for a smoke and a rest and went to see about our own breakfast. First of all we had a gorgeous hot bath in a princely bathroom with big sponges and taps that roared like the Atlantic Ocean and shiny nickel fittings and showers and warmed Turkish towels and scented soap (different from a bath in the distressful country, I'm afraid) and then, after having our hair cut out and shampooed, our faces shaved; our boots polished, and putting on clean underclothes and socks, we felt real good, and went in to all the things we can't get in the mess, and ate a breakfast that scandalised even the head waiter.

Shining with soap and repletion, we came out at last, and strolled heavily across to put the men in the train for the last lap, and despatched a final telegram ahead to order a transport wagon from the regiment to meet us at the station.

It was a slow train, and it wasn't until twelve o'clock that we reached Frimley. Here we tumbled out, loaded up all our stuff into the wagon, and started to march the two or three miles up to Blackdown Camp

We got here about half-past one, and handed over our reports, accounts, and marching-in roll to the C.O., and dismissed the men with a profound feeling of thankfulness and wrote 'finis' to the show. I couldn't help thinking how differently the men behaved from the first draft that came down from Galway...

Finn [author's dog] travelled over quite all right with me. He came as a recruit, so I didn't pay a penny for him. I had something else to do than bother about dog-tickets.

Bed-time. Good-night."

Corporal Francis Mack, a young man from New South Wales was a volunteer in the ANZACs (Australia and New Zealand Auxiliary Corps) and served with the 29th Battalion Australian Infantry. It is clear from his letters that, although he was aware of the serious nature of the war, he took every opportunity to enjoy what seemed to be a great adventure 10,000 miles from home. The letters from his family took around two months to reach him, and he regales them with tales of wartime London and the rather more somber experiences of life in the trenches.

"England   27th January, 1917

Dear Mother and Father,

Just back from leave in London. I had a real roaring time. The time (4 days) was rather short. I managed to see most of the old ancient and historical sights. I was somehow disappointed in London after reading so much about it—really expected to see something more impressive than it is. Mind you, we see London now at its worst for everything is in darkness at 5pm in the afternoon so the days were terribly short. I went to see the Tower of London, Buckingham Palace, Whitehall, The War Office, Westminster Abbey, St. Paul's Cathedral, Trafalgar Square, Leicester Square, Piccadilly Circus, Bond Street and other places too numerous to mention. These sights are grand—there are no two ways about that but the rest, the business houses and eating places are only commonplace. The big difference between Sydney and London is the trams. London has no trams through the streets—they all run underground and are all privately owned. There are two classes of trams—the Tube and the Electric Line. The Tube is a way—it Billy O down—say 5 or 600 feet down while the Electric is only about 50 feet. They are very cheap and extra fast. On the streets run O'Buses (Motor) after the style of the trams. There are thousands—you can see them everywhere and these were very attractive to see. You wonder why. Well, firstly you can see London better from an omnibus than anything else and secondly but none the least important is that the conductor is a Girl. That's a thing which struck us as peculiar, girls doing all sorts of jobs, walk down the street and you see a window cleaner. I had seen photos of them in papers but had I not seen them I would not have believed it. But never the less they were there dressed in men's clothes of oilskin.

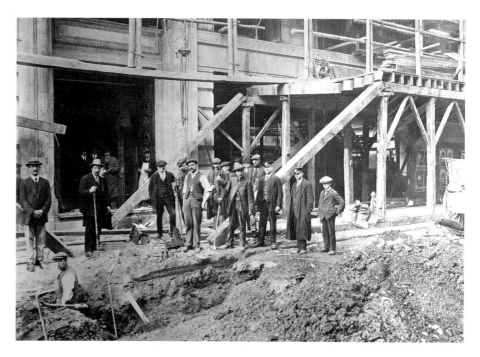

Above and below: These two picture show the damage wrought by German Zeppelin raids over London. The raids began in May 1915 and were usually carried out on moonlit nights. London's defenses were swiftly improved, but it was not until September 2, 1916, that the first Zeppelin was shot down over Middlesex.

Go a bit further and you see a girl page, girl done up in livery to put it plainly, girls are doing everything.

We had theatre parties every evening for there is nothing else to do, it is so dark. Another thing, go in for dinner and after having soup and joints they won't serve you with sweets and when you get your bill they charge for each thing separately. Oh! the difference from Australia. Take a tip from me stay in New South. Sydney is not too bad at all. I was stopping at a friend's peoples place at Kensington, West London and they treated us right royally. London is the thing for the cash. 4 days—$4/10/—not bad going eh? Well that is all our leave so I made the best of it. Well I can't remember much more now to tell so must close. Tell Mr Cook I went round to see his brother but they couldn't find him and I couldn't wait too long as time is precious while on leave.

They have shifted from Horsferry Road and are in a Hall not far from the HeadQuarters, was sorry I missed him. I hope everything at home is OK and that you all are in the best of health. Remember me to relatives and friends. I haven't received many letters from relatives so you can give them my news as it is hard to settle down to write in such cold weather.

I'll answer all letters I receive so if anyone wants to hear from me direct, it's up to them to write now and again. I am not too bad. I have had, and in fact I still have a very bad cold and terribly sore feet from walking over the hard frozen ground. Otherwise I am splendid. Well mother must close. Am sending you some views of London and the places I have visited together with some English papers. Well goodbye mother and father, sisters and brothers. Fondest love to you all.

I remain yours, am luckily your loving son,
Frank."

Above right: An Allied officer leads the way among bursting German shells during the Arras and Cambrai offensive, April 7, 1918.

Right: German storm troops laden with equipment go over the top to open and broken ground. In 1918, the Sturmgruppen were responsible for the advances of the Ludendorff Offensive.

Nearly a year later, Frank's unit was in the front line, enduring the hell of winter in the trenches.

"France.
2-1-18.

Dear Mother & Father,

Just a line or two to start the New Year. We have had a pretty fair time during this spell. New Year as you can quite imagine was not without its bit of jollification "Compree"—in fact some of the boys had a great liking to the Champagne Vin Mulago etc. Champagne was favorite for it is so cheap here. But one can make allowances for the exuberant spirit of the few under the conditions we are in. I'll now try and give you some idea of our last trip up to Fritz. First we are billeted several miles from the line—from here we tramp with full wardrobe on back to a like 2 miles or more behind the line where we take up residence in dugouts & are well within shell fire. At midday we go digging a cable for the artillery. This is digging frozen ground with snow frozen hand. Here you stay for say 7 days then pick up your bed & walk (at night in pitch darkness) over and in & out "Duckboard track"— like a ladder on rungs together for about 3 miles—rifle, ammunition, rations, clothes, water. We arrive platoon at a time at our destination & this is 'Supports'. We again get our dugouts & right away we get to work. 2 a.m pulled out on fatigue to take hot soup up to the line. Imagine this trip, 1000 yds off the line, pitch dark no regular track & ground torn up by shells. We wore thigh high gum boots & as there is so much traffic at night that for half way it is a sea of mud—a party of 10 men getting through this knee deep mud when out rattles Fritz's machine gun—down we all go—mud is far nicer than lead. Every time a Star shell goes up & lights the whole place up you have to stand—not budge an inch. Tis grand this 1000 yds—takes an hour & a half—3 hours for the whole trip. Next night we get a change—sleep at day of course and out at dusk—this time tis raining and we are to mine No-man's Land—pouring rain and we are creeping along on our way to the job which of course has to be without noise—tis a great sensation to be laying in the mud and listening to Fritz spraying over the

top of you with his machine guns. We get home at Midnight—mud head to foot and wet thro with not the slightest hope of drying your clothes which means for the next two days you are damp. And so the work goes on—fatigues—why would break a man's heart they come so constant. No-one who hasn't been thro the mill can have any idea what it is like. From here you go and do your turn in the line for 3 days and well this is putting you on pins and needles all the time tho sleep is soon the master and you can sleep thro all the noise of the day for from dusk till daybreak all hands stand to. Coming out the second time in we got spotted relieving and Fritz caught a couple of platoons in his barrage. Our platoon only had 2 casualties for we were lucky enough to be just behind it doing a shiver. I mean [...censored...]. Tis hardly necessary to mention it but should you receive any news of me don't forget to pass it on to Menangle Mother for am sure they would like to know of it. Am Dinkum there you know so Don't forget. Well Mother nothing more to say at present.

Fondest love,
I Remain Yr. Loving Son
Frank."

America rode out most of World War I on an isolationist cloud of neutrality: "neutral in thought, word, and deed," as President Woodrow Wilson said. But when, in 1917, the Germans extended their submarine warfare to attack any ship from any nation which dared to approach the British Isles, the U.S.A. felt impelled to declare war. Although the bulk of American troops did not actually arrive in France until March 1918, American entry into the war boosted flagging British and French morale. They were on the defensive, their resources of men and matériel severely depleted, and the American Expeditionary Force under General Pershing, provided two million fresh troops before the war's end.

Kansas-born Lloyd Staley volunteered for service with the U.S. Army in August 1917 and served with the 137th U.S. Infantry, 35th Division, which was formed by recruits from Kansas and Missouri. They arrived in England in May 1918, arriving in France on May 9. Lloyd had the good fortune to work in the Postal Detachment, and was perhaps spared the worst excesses of front line soldiering.

"May 29, 1918
My Dearest Mary,

I received my first mail since I have gotten across yesterday. Two letters from you are dated April 19 and the other April 22. The first one was written before you had heard my N.Y. address and the other was addressed to Camp Mills. They were indeed highly appreciated letters and I believe that I can look for more right soon as the mail has begun to come now. There were two other letters for me also; one from Mother and Ethel, the other from James. The last was of the most recent date: May 6. This was certainly an excited company when we found out there was so much mail for us. Almost everyone got at least one letter and a few were as fortunate as myself.

I was rather surprised to hear that Robert was going into the R.F.C. [Royal Flying Corps] although you had told me of it, too. But to know that he had already left for camp and by the time you get this letter he will probably be in England was just a bit of a surprise. Well, I am glad that he is in the service but, of course, I would like to have seen him in a uniform of the U.S.A. It is all one cause, however, and we are comrades just the same whether American, English, or what. I have seen some mighty fine men from Britain just what short time I have been here. (My pen went dry and I haven't any ink at my elbow as I did in U.S.)

Speaking of the English, it is wonderful how men can go through three and four years of this war and still be smiling, cheerful, good-natured fellows, but they are. I agree with Robert when he says there will be two classes of men in America after the war—the ones who went, and the ones who did not. And I believe as he does the ones who went are going to be the ones who will have charge of affairs when they get back for, if a man stands this war and still comes out smiling, he is a man. I certainly hope I may have a chance of seeing Robert over here but it would be only an accident I am afraid.

Let me know his address from time to time so if there is any way of seeing him, I will do all I can to find him.

You must have a nice home now and right in your old neighborhood. And those fruit trees take my eye. I believe I could consume your total production right now. Some of these times we will sample that fruit and also stroll over to Swope Park and look things over considerably after the war, après la guerre, as the French say. When ever you say anything to them about certain things they can't do now, they always say "after the war," and I think that little expression shows to what extremes they are willing to go in self sacrifice. I certainly have a very high opinion of the French. They are most highly respected by the American soldiers and they return the compliment.

To sit here where I am now, it seems scarcely possible that we are so near the front. This country here is a peaceful-looking farming country and, to look out over the quiet fields, it is hard to realize that the fighting is so close at hand. To walk across these fields is just like taking a stroll over Dad's farm on some quiet Sunday afternoon. Only there are several things that are conspicuously absent—most of all the folks that were left behind. The ones that you love and are loved by is what goes to make life worthwhile.

Well, the sound of the big guns somewhere not so many miles away has begun again. Sometimes the sound comes from one side, then the other, until it is hard to tell which way one could go and not find someone shooting at someone else. My address is the same: Co. K, 137th Inf., Amer. E.F. I expect you know it by this time but some of my letters may drop by the wayside so it is best to be sure for I certainly want to get all the mail that is coming to me.

So, goodbye to the little girl who has given up two loved ones so cheerfully and sent them away with the smile that counts.

With sincerest love, Lloyd"
[Reprinted courtesy Jeffrey Lloyd Staley]

Left: The SS *Mauritania* arrives with the first batch of American soldiers. American entry into the war boosted flagging British and French morale.

Corporal Roy Bainbridge had a less peaceful time and found himself in the thick of fighting. American troops made a crucial difference to the caliber of fighting in 1918. Unlike their French and British comrades they were fresh, enthusiastic, and less wary of the Germans, simply because they had not witnessed three demoralizing years of slaughter at close hand. As Bainbridge notes, however, the Americans relied on local knowledge and experience to start with.

"July 18th 1918

Dear Mother,
Well there has been great activity in the line of warfare since my last letter. I never realized before that destruction of material things as well as human life could possibly occur in a few hours. Just a few days ago we witnessed the greatest artillery fire, and also its effect, since the war began.

...The work done in the section in which we were located in the winter and early spring was child's play compared to the works at present. But it is full of excitement and therefore we like it.

One afternoon on the first day of this offensive, I and twelve of fifteen of the men in our company, were left in camp while the rest of the company were out delivering ammunition. Long range guns were scoring a few direct hits on the hospital. Now it is very seldom you hear the guns that fire these long range shells but on this occasion we could hear the guns that were firing these shells. The report could be heard before the shell comes over. And the sound could be distinguished from the sound of the hundred other guns which were firing continually. About three seconds after the report the gun was heard then come the short shell whine or whistle of the shell going over then the explosion itself. These shells were falling only about three hundred yards over and beyond us and were going directly over us. We didn't feel much danger as its shells were going over and anyway there were few dugouts in this town so we came out lying on the grass. But later these gunners became careless with their range and shells started to drop first on one side and then another. We became interested immediately.

The French told us to lie in the ditch beside a small narrow gauge railway that ran nearby. About the time we got in there it seemed as if Fritz started to find this road with his shells. So we just kept moving from one spot to another until we decided that a nearby wheat field was the place to go. I never saw Fritz waste any shells on a wheat field. Here we felt pretty safe and we watched the shells as they dropped on as among the buildings.

Every time we heard the whistle of a coming shell we would duck just the same. This whine of the coming shell can be heard two or three seconds before it hits. This depends upon the direction of the wind and distance away from where the shell hits. If the shell goes over the sound is longer.

It is certainly a helpless feeling that comes upon one when the shells come near and you are out in the open, on an open road, or halted on a shell swept road that is filled with traffic.

I am not writing this to show you the danger because all this does not happen every day and we have not lost a man so far in this offensive. The area of ground is so large that thousands of shells do nothing but dig holes in the ground. It is a very small percent that actually does any damage.

Well I believe we are about due for some mail. It has been several weeks since I have received any. Write a little more often if possible.

Give my love to Bob and Bertha.

Your son
Corp. R. T. Bainbridge
117 Am. Train Co C
American E.F."

Private Fred Cavin of Virginia wrote home to his sister a month after the Armistice, describing the fighting in the Argonne Woods in September, one of the last and bloodiest offensives of the war. He mentions the appalling Spanish influenza which swept across Europe after the war, killing millions of people.

"Dec. 15, 1918
Etraye France

Dear Sister
I just received your letter of Nov. 27, and as I have time I will answer immediately. I have been on the front twice and as Joe Nugent wrote home and told his people I suppose I may as well tell you. He is in the 314 Inf. which is in the same Div. that I am in the 79th. We have a fighting Div. and we made a good name for ourselves and we get lots of write ups in the papers.

My first time in the trenches was a week in Sept. On the 26th of Sept the morning the big Allied drive started my outfit went over the top on the Verdun Sector. We captured Mont Faucon the first day after some hard fighting. We captured and killed lots of Germans and

Right: A French soldier falls after being shot in no-man's-land near Verdun. French troops eventually broke through the German lines in December 1916, but some 700,000 men had died in the battle for Verdun.

I with another fellow captured four Germans and a machine gun. We then pushed on until we ran into the Argonne Woods where we fought for two days. We were then relieved by the third division I was certainly glad we did get relieved when we did, for the Argonne Woods was a regular slaughter house. We were on that drive for five days and nights All of us were cold, hungry, wet and could just about stand on our feet. Two days after we were relieved I had to be hauled to the hospital. I was in the hospital for three weeks with the Spanish Flu and believe me I was sick. I was discharged from the hospital the later part of Oct. and sent back to my outfit.

When I met my company they were just starting on another drive and we also had a hot reception on it. I will tell you about it some other time for you know I am not much of a hand at writing long letters. After all that I have gone through I think I am one of the luckiest fellows in the world. I am surely glad this thing is over it gave us a chance to get washed up and rid of the cooties. I suppose you think it is strange to hear me talking about having cooties but I was alive with them twice. They were a very common thing for the dough boys who were on the front. I will try and bring a souvenir for you when I come back to the states and I hope it will be soon I will close now I am well and hope all of you are the same.

Fred

Pvt. Fred W. Cavin
Co. M 315 Inf.
Amer. E.F.
A.P.O. 771

Censored by Lt. GN

Tell Nell that I received the money orders O.K."

Harry S. Truman, vice president for most of World War II and president after Roosevelt's death in April 1945, spent the Great War as an artillery captain. A member of the National Guard in Kansas since 1905, he was promoted to sergeant and very quickly commissioned a lieutenant when America joined the war in 1917. Truman's unit, the 129th Field Artillery, 35th Division was shipped to France in February 1918. He wrote devotedly

Right: "It isn't as bad as I thought it would be but it's bad enough," wrote Harry S. Truman in 1918. Truman was an artillery captain during World War I and served in France 1918–1919.

to his fiancée Bess Wallace throughout his time abroad, but this letter, written on the day the Armistice was declared is particularly interesting. Truman reflects the feelings of many of his comrades who were intent on inflicting as much pain on the Germans (or "Heinie") as they could. Firing continued right up until the time of the carefully chosen ceasefire, at the 11th hour, of the 11th day of the 11th month, 1918.

"Dear Bess: November 11, 1918

...Their time for acceptance will be up in thirty minutes. There is a great big 155 Battery right behind me across the road that seems to want to get rid of all of its ammunition before the time is up. It has been banging away almost as fast as a 75 Battery for the last two hours. Every time one of the guns goes off it shakes my house like an earthquake.

I just got official notice that hostilities would cease at eleven o'clock. Every one is about to have a fit. I fired 164 rounds at him before he quit this morning anyway. It seems that everyone was just about to blow up wondering if Heinie would come in. I knew that Germany could not stand the gaff. For all their preparedness and swashbuckling talk they cannot stand adversity. France was whipped for four years and never gave up and one good licking suffices for Germany. What pleases me most is the fact that I was lucky enough to take a Battery through the last drive. The Battery has shot something over ten thousand rounds at the Hun and I am sure they had a slight effect...

You evidently did some very excellent work as a Liberty bond saleswoman because I saw in The Stars and Stripes where some twenty-two million people bought them and that they were oversubscribed by $1 billion, which is some stunt for you to have helped pull off. I know that it had as much to do with breaking the German morale as our cannon shots had and we owe you as much for an early homecoming as we do the fighters.

Here's hoping to see you soon.

Yours always,

Harry"

105

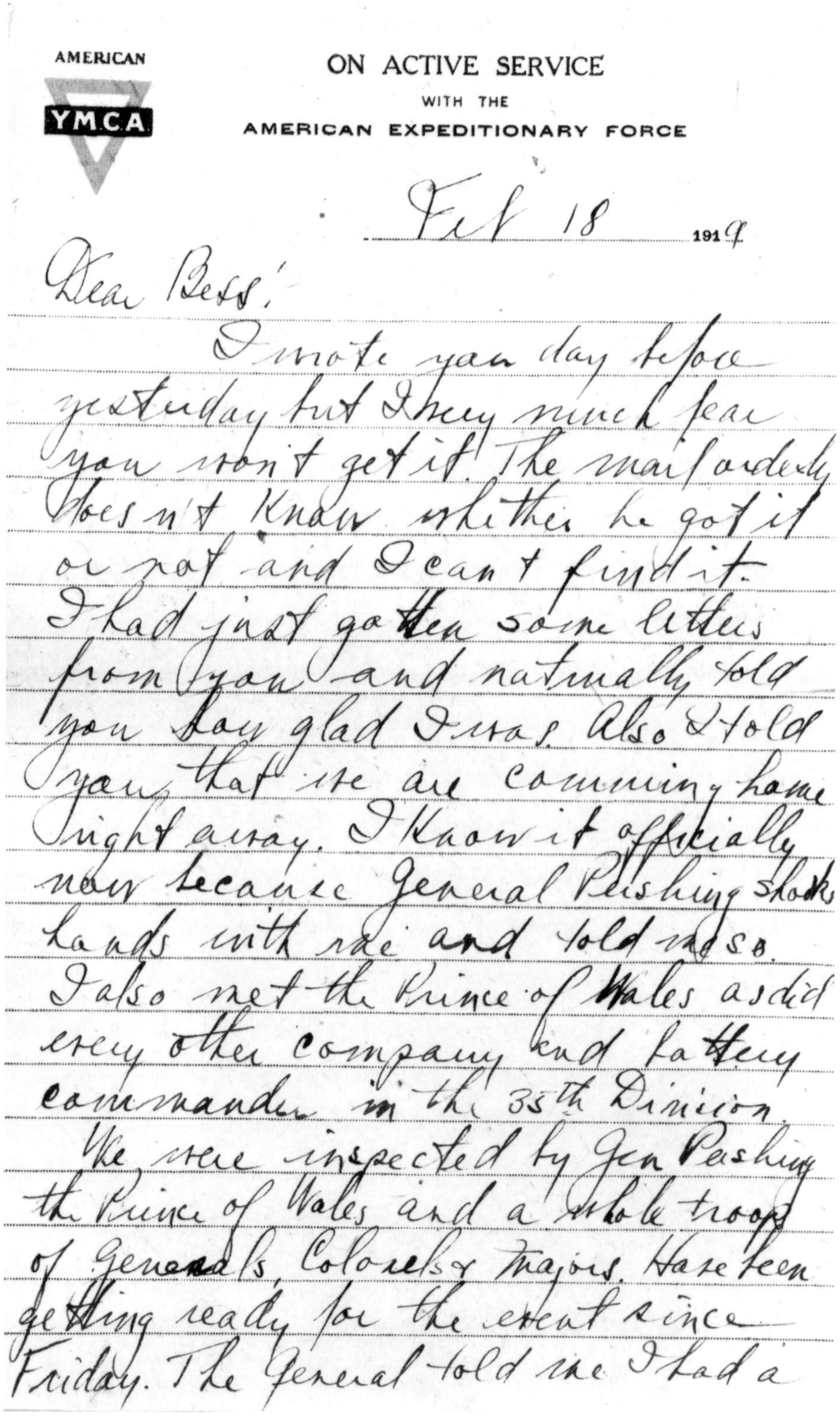

In February 1919, Truman received the news all soldiers long for: they were going home. His letter to his fiancée bubbles with joy and excitement, buoyed up by his plans for the future.

[Rosieres, near Bar-le-Duc]

"Dear Bess: February 18, 1919

I wrote you day before yesterday but I very much fear you won't get it. The mail orderly doesn't know whether he got it or not and I can't find it. I had just gotten some letters from you and naturally told you how glad I was. Also I told you that we are coming home right away. I know it officially now because General Pershing shook hands with me—and told me so. I also met the Prince of Wales, as did every other company and battery commander in the 35th Division... Please get ready to march down the aisle with me just as soon as you decently can when I get back. I haven't any place to go but home and I'm busted financially but I love you as madly as a man can and I'll find all the other things. We'll be married anywhere you say at any time you mention and if you want only one person or the whole town I don't care as long as you make it quickly after my arrival. I have some army friends I'd like to ask and my own family and that's all I care about, and the army friends can go hang if you don't want 'em. I have enough money to buy a Ford and we can set sail in that and arrive in Happyland at once and quickly.

Don't fail to write just 'cause I'm starting home.

Yours always,

Harry"

Left: Copy of original letter sent by Harry S. Truman to his sweetheart Bess.

Far left: A Russian soldier writes a letter home. After many hours marching, the soldiers have removed their boots.

MR. MARTIN

We have been asked whether there is any official ruling or practice as to the proper way to describe the last war and the present war.   The phrase "Great War" certainly seems pretty inappropriate now.

The alternatives which first occur to one are:

"War of 1914-18" and "War of 1939-4?"

"First World War" and "Second World War"

"Four Years' War" and "Five (or six, or seven)
Years' War".

Has the Prime Minister a view as to the form of words he would prefer to be used?

EEB

24th June, 1944

Right: British civil servants wrote to Winston Churchill's private secretary asking for the prime minister's thoughts on the official names for the world wars. Churchill circled and initialed the second option.

World War II 1939–1945

By the mid 1930s, it became clear that World War I, the "war to end all wars," had not lived up to its reputation. Unquestionably terrible, World War I appeared to have created as many problems as it solved. Humiliated, angered, and impoverished by punitive war reparations, Germany became poisoned by a nationalism so strong, that Fascism flourished and became the norm throughout German society. The League of Nations, established by the Treaty of Versailles in 1919, was a well-meaning but essentially emasculated body that had scant success in controlling the excesses of aggrandizing countries.

In 1939, the appeasement of Germany's expansionist policies had clearly failed. The German invasion in 1938 of part of Czechoslovakia (the Sudetenland) and annexation of Austria—apparently Hitler's last territorial claim in Europe—had not satisfied his plans for a greater Reich. When Poland was invaded and Belgium threatened in September 1939, Britain and France declared war. The German Blitzkrieg in the spring of 1940, a masterpiece of military maneuvering, yielded Belgium, the Netherlands, and France to the forces of the Reich. Most of the British Expeditionary Force was evacuated from Dunkirk, along with many French soldiers, but they left behind a great deal of matériel and equipment. Hitler dominated Europe and only Britain survived to oppose him, although the country was in a poor state to do so. In alliance with Italy, the Germans took the war to Greece and the Balkans and then to North Africa. In June 1941, Hitler turned on the Soviet Union, ignoring the Nazi-Soviet Pact of 1939, which was a treaty of nonaggression, and unleashing Operation Barbarossa, the invasion of the Soviet Union.

Meanwhile, having seized Manchuria from China in 1937 and occupied several major cities and ports, Japan had its own territorial ambitions in the Far East. A war between the European powers diverted resources from their colonies and encouraged Japanese plans for an empire in Southeast Asia. After the attack on Pearl Harbor in December 1941, Japanese forces swept south across Malaya, the Dutch East Indies, the Philippines, and Burma, ejecting the British, Dutch, and French from their colonial possessions with brutal force. The Americans began the slow battle to recover Japanese conquests, relentlessly pursuing the Japanese on two fronts, across the Pacific, and north from New Guinea to the Philippines.

It was a truly global conflict that left nowhere untouched. In 1944, shortly after the D-Day landings in France, British civil servants wrote to Churchill's private secretary asking for the prime minister's thoughts on the official name for the conflagration:

> "We have been asked whether there is any official ruling or practice as to the proper way to describe the last war and the present war. The phrase "Great War" certainly seems pretty inappropriate now.
>
> The alternatives which first occur to one are:
> "War of 1914–18" and "War of 1939–4?"
> "First World War" and "Second World War"
> "Four Years' War" and "Five (or six, or seven) Years' War".
>
> Has the Prime Minister a view as to the form of words he would prefer to be used?"
>
> [Churchill circled the second option.]

Britain seriously began preparing for war in the mid-1930s, increasing armament production, introducing civil defense measures, and after the Munich crisis of 1938, considering plans for conscription.

Lieutenant John Stillwell served with the Territorial Unit, 44th Battalion, 5th Royal Tank Regiment in North Africa. During the late 1930s he had been a "weekend soldier," and was called up in 1940. In March 1941, his unit was shipped to Egypt, making the long journey around Africa. He wrote home to his wife who was expecting their first child, whom John hoped would be a girl, (although his wife felt otherwise). When he wrote this letter he had been away from home for six months, and had recently taken part in the British advance from Egypt into Libya.

"44th BN RTR
MEF
27.9.41

My Precious Darling
I do hope you have not been worrying through mail being interrupted for 14 days back, truth is this is honestly and truly the first time I have sat down long enough to write for a fortnight. We have been on the move and travelled quite a long way one way and another. I am now sitting in a very beautifully dug trench about 3ft deep and with my bivouac rigged over it. I can just sit down inside at my table to write this evening. Perkins [the batman] removes my table and chair and my bed fits in beautifully, so my sleep is quite undisturbed. Perkins has worked hard at the digging and we made one or two improvements and am now getting comfy. Poor chap, he does hate having to move from one place to another. No bathing now unfortunately, as water is strictly limited to gallon a day for all purposes, but I still wash my feet every day. Am very fit myself—really got my face rather sunburnt through travelling in one direction for a long period. It is only on the left side, though.

Darling Angel, the best birthday present I could ever receive from you arrived today and did it cheer me up? At last, it was your photos sent in May and a letter of May 21st and also an AMPC of 2/8/41. Jan, the photos are marvellous—you do look so sweet and that dear little curl at the side, I cannot get over it. Thank you so much darling, frame is very nice and just the right size to fit in my pack.

Your letters fill in quite lot of gaps in the news and I must read them again when I have finished this. Had a letter from Jim too—was good of him. I was sorry to hear he had impetigo—horrid thing isn't it? I expect you will soon be starting fires, and I hope you have a big store of logs ready. So disappointing to have a miserable August. I hate it when it ought to be hot. Weather is most peculiar

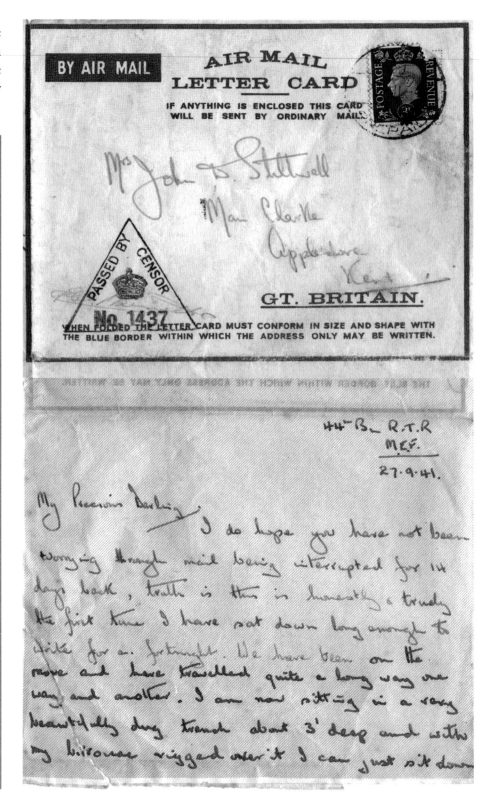

110

here, now it is cold in the morning and evening, so that you want your battle dress top on, and during the day boiling hot. I am wearing my KD [khaki drill] slacks as it keeps my knees warm and clean too—washing clothes is rather a snag but Perkins managed to do everything while I was away for three days on a job collecting things we had left behind while moving.

Darling Jan, the time is getting short now, I do hope you are not suffering any pain or trouble with Eliza Ann. I am sure she will be a model baby and never disturb you at nights, she wouldn't have the nerve to without me there to rock her to sleep again. I have a bottle of booze ready to open when I get the wire with the news. Have you done anything about godparents and so on? Let me know won't you.

Do love you so much darling one. Look after yourself.

Cheerio

Love
John"

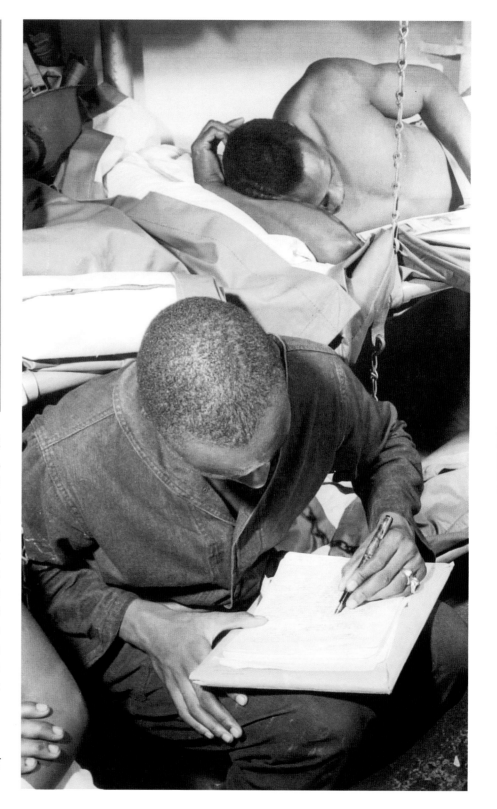

In 1941, it seemed that only Britain and the forces of the Empire survived to defend democracy against the forces of the Reich. Desperate for support, Britain hoped that the U.S.A. (officially neutral until December 7, 1941) would join the war, yet in June 1941, as this next document shows, the British worried about matters of security to the point of paranoia, and were reluctant to share military intelligence. Once in possession of the Enigma codes, which enabled them to intercept U-boat signals, it was crucial that they did not betray their knowledge to the Germans, and so the hesitation in allowing the U.S.A. to know the extent of British intelligence on the subject is perhaps understandable. However, despite the fact that Britain was enduring perhaps the darkest hours of the war, this letter is imbued with a peculiarly British sense of sang-froid and superiority. This memo was written two days after the Germans invaded Russia and one wonders whether British signals intelligence was aware of the Germans' intentions before the Soviet Union did.

Right: A sailor in the bunkroom aboard the USS *Ticonderoga* looks at pictures of his children, while a bunkmate writes a letter home.

HW 1/6

OST SECRET

C/6863.

LONDON,

24th June, 1941.

PRIME MINISTER.

After considering, from all angles, the possibility of divulging to the President the information regarding U.S. Naval Units being chased by U. Boats, I find myself unable to devise any safe means of wrapping up the information in a manner which would not imperil this source, which should, without fail, play a vital part in the Battle of the Atlantic.

The fact that the message in question was passed by the Admiral Commanding U. Boats to submarines actually operating, renders it well nigh impossible that the informatic could have been secured by an agent, and however much we insist that it came from a highly placed source, I greatly doubt the enemy being for a moment deceived, should there be any indiscretion in the U.S.A. That this might occur, cannot be ruled out, as the Americans are not in any sense as security minded as one would wish, and I need only draw your attention to the attached cutting from to-day's "Daily Express" on a matter which, in my opinion, should not have been made public if the two Secret Services are to work together as closely as is imperative.

It is true that the American experts who visited the United Kingdom gave us a very valuable insight into Japanese cryptographic methods, but they, themselves, impresse upon me how cautious they were in passing any of the results to the State Department.

At a recent Meeting of the Chiefs of Staff, it was agreed that information derived from this Most Secret source should only be communicated to the U.S. Naval and Military Authorities when we were satisfied that the source was not endangered. I believe that any other decision as regards weakening the veil of secrecy would cause the greatest regret at a later date, and I similarly hold the view that it would be fatal to divulge to the Russians immediate information which we are securing about German operational intentions on the Eastern Front. To be of any value, it would mean that the information would be immediately transmitted to the Commanders

in/

"24 June 1941

Prime Minister,

After considering, from all angles, the possibility of divulging to the President the information regarding U.S. Naval Units being chased by U. Boats, I find myself unable to devise any safe means of wrapping up the information in a manner which would not imperil this source, which should, without fail, play a vital part in the battle of the Atlantic.

The fact that the message in question was passed by the Admiral Commanding U. Boats to submarines actually operating, renders it well nigh impossible that the information could have been secured by an agent, and however much we insist that it came from a highly placed source, I greatly doubt the enemy being for a moment deceived, should there be any indiscretion in the U.S.A. That this might occur, cannot be ruled out, as the Americans are not in any sense as security minded as one would wish...

It is true that American security experts who visited the United Kingdom gave us a very valuable insight into Japanese cryptographic methods, but they, themselves, impressed upon me how cautious they were in passing any of the results to the State Department.

At a recent Meeting of the Chiefs of Staff, it was agreed that information derived from this Most Secret source should only be communicated to the U.S. Naval and Military Authorities when we were satisfied that the source was not endangered. I believe that any other decision as regards weakening the veil of secrecy would cause the greatest regret at a later date, and I similarly hold the view that it would be fatal to divulge to the Russians immediate information which we are securing about German operational intentions on the Eastern Front. To be of any value, it would mean that the information would be immediately transmitted to the Commanders in the Field, and as the Russian military cyphers are compromised, it would only be a matter of days before the Germans knew of our success, and operations in the future would almost certainly be hidden in an unbreakable way."

The Japanese swept through the Far East like a typhoon, with the outposts of the empire falling like skittles. They were far better equipped for jungle warfare than the British, whose defense was founded on outdated methods better suited to European warfare. Finally in February 1942, Singapore was threatened and General Wavell issued a strongly worded last order to the troops which reflected entirely the inflexible imperialist attitude of the British high command.

"10th February 1942

It is certain that our troops on Singapore, heavily outnumber any Japanese troops who have crossed the straits. We must destroy them. Our whole fighting reputation is at stake and the honour of the British Empire. The Americans had held out in the Batan Peninsula against far heavier odds. The Russians are turning back the picked strength of the Germans. The Chinese with almost complete lack of modern equipment have held the Japanese for four and half years. It will be disgraceful if we cannot hold our boasted Fortress of Singapore to inferior enemy forces. There must be no thought of sparing the troops or the Civilian population, and no mercy must be shown in any shape or form. Commanders and Senior Officers must lead their troops, and if necessary, die with them. There must be no thought of surrender, and every unit must fight it out to the end, and in close contact with the enemy. Please see that the above is brought to the attention of all Senior Officers and through them to all troops. I look to you and your men to fight to the end, to prove that the fighting spirit that won our Empire shall and still exists to defend it.

Signed

Wavell
General C-in-C Southern Pacific"

His orders could not have been plainer, but they contrast rather sharply with the more pragmatic (and considerably less wasteful of human resources) memo written five days later by Lieutenant General A. E. Percival, the commander in Singapore.

"15th February 1942

It has been necessary to give up the struggle, but I want the reason explained to all ranks. The forward troops continue to hold their ground but the essentials of war have run short. In a few days we shall have neither petrol nor food. Many types of ammunition are short and the water supply on which the vast civilian population and many of the fighting troops are dependent, threatens to fail. The situation has been brought about, partly by being driven off our dumps and by hostile artillery and air action. Without these sinews of war, we cannot fight on.

I thank all ranks for their efforts throughout the campaign,
A.E. Percival Lieut. General
Malaya Command"

Right: Soldiers of the Royal Tank Regiment take a break to play cards in the heat of the Western Desert, North Africa, during World War II.

A number of innovations were made to reduce the weight of mailbags during World War II. Lightweight air letters were issued to British troops in North Africa at the rate of one a month, although more could be purchased. Airgraphs (for the British), or V-Mail (to the Americans), were small letters written on preprinted forms which were then photographed. After a letter had been written and censored, it was microfilmed. One small, lightweight roll of film containing hundreds of letters was flown home where the letters were printed on photographic paper, put in an envelope, and sent to the addressee through the normal postal system. Airgraphs usually reached their destinations more quickly than airmail, but for the British at least, were a more expensive means of communication. There was only a small amount of space in which to write, and special forms were printed at Christmas for use as substitute Christmas cards.

> "21.2.42
>
> Dear Major Stillwell
>
> I must apologise that your card has not been answered before now, but you will appreciate, I am sure, that present conditions are to blame for the delay.
>
> I am taking this rather quicker means of communication to tell you that a letter is on its way to you by airmail, giving you all the details we can about the whole circumstances of John's death, which we feel must now be accepted as certain.
>
> Both for the work that he did and as a personality he is a great loss to the battalion. I am pleased to say that his batman, Perkins is quite safe and is still with us.
>
> Your sincerely,
> PW Larman
> Capt. 44 RTR"

After Pearl Harbor, the U.S.A. marshaled its forces for the long fight to recapture the islands of the Pacific and Southeast Asia. In 1942, 25-year-old Jack Kennedy joined the U.S. Navy and in September returned home for a short period of leave. The good-luck trinket he refers to in the letter seems to have worked. The following summer, Kennedy and the crew of his PT boat were injured when their craft was rammed by a Japanese destroyer near

Above: Airgraphs, or V-mails, usually reached their destination more quickly than airmail, but only gave a limited amount of space in which to write. Special forms were printed at Christmas, such as this one, and were used as substitute Christmas cards.

the Pacific island of New Georgia. Shortly afterward Kennedy wrote to Claire Booth Luce, with his customary charm, thanking her again for the lucky coin: "With it goes my sincere thanks for your good-luck piece, which did service above and beyond its routine duties during a rather busy period."

"A Hyannisport
Massachusetts

Sept 29 [1942]

Dear Miss Luce,
I came home yester-day and dad gave me your letter with the gold coin. The coin is now fastened to my identification tag and will be there, I hope, for the duration.

   I couldn't have been more pleased. Good luck is a commodity in rather large demand these days and I feel you have given me a particularly potent bit of it. The fact that it once belonged to your Mother —and then to you and you were good enough and thought enough to pass it along to me—has made me especially happy to have it.

   Just before coming home, I was considering getting a St Christopher medal to wear. Now, however, for me St Christophers are out—I'll string along with my St Claire.

Sincerely,

Jack Kennedy"

Kansas-born John Martin served with U.S. forces in the Pacific during the dual-pronged campaign to recapture Japanese-occupied territories. Martin served on the more southerly offensive, fighting from New Guinea across the Solomon Islands and on to the Philippines. These two short letters convey something of the conditions on New Guinea—hot, humid, muddy, and mosquito-infested. The first epistle was a V-mail.

Right: The letter from Claire Booth Luce, a family friend of the young John Kennedy.

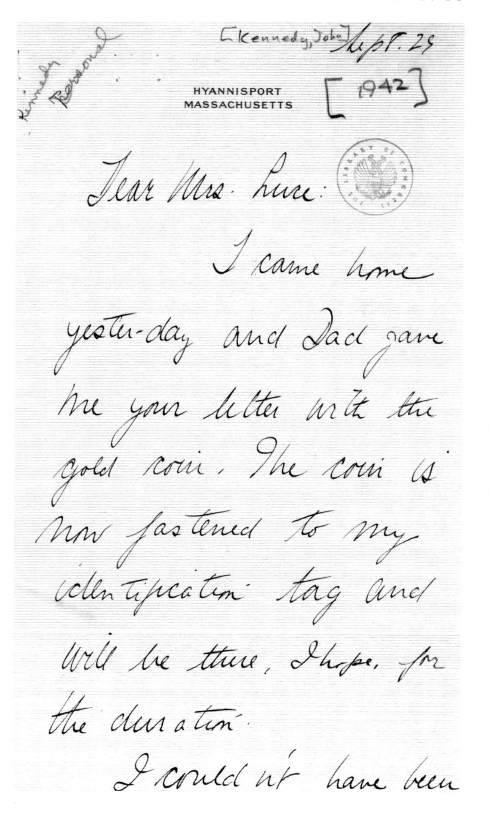

"28 Apr. '44

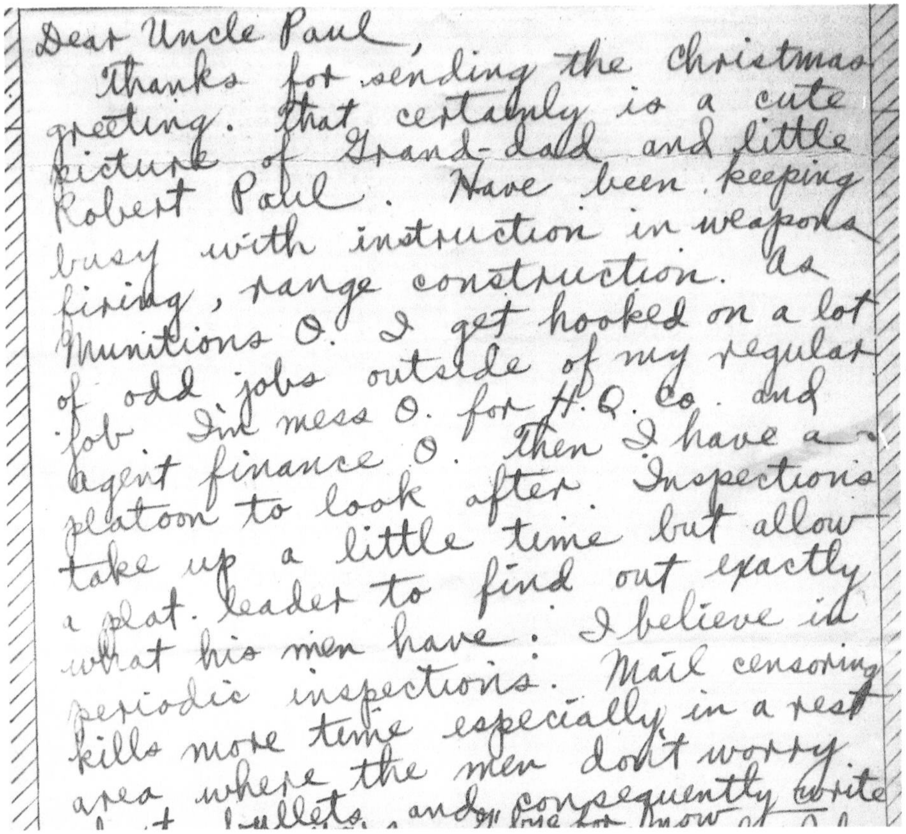

Dear Uncle Paul,

Thanks for sending the Christmas greeting. That certainly is a cute picture of Grand-dad and little Robert Paul. Have been keeping busy with instruction in weapons firing, range construction. As munitions O[fficer] I get hooked on a lot of odd jobs outside of my regular job. I'm mess O[fficer] for H.Q. Co. and agent finance O[fficer] then I have a platoon to look after. Inspections take up a little time but allow a plat[oon] leader to find out exactly what his men have. I believe in periodic inspections. Mail censoring kills more time especially in a rest area where the men don't worry about bullets and consequently write plenty of letters. Bye for now

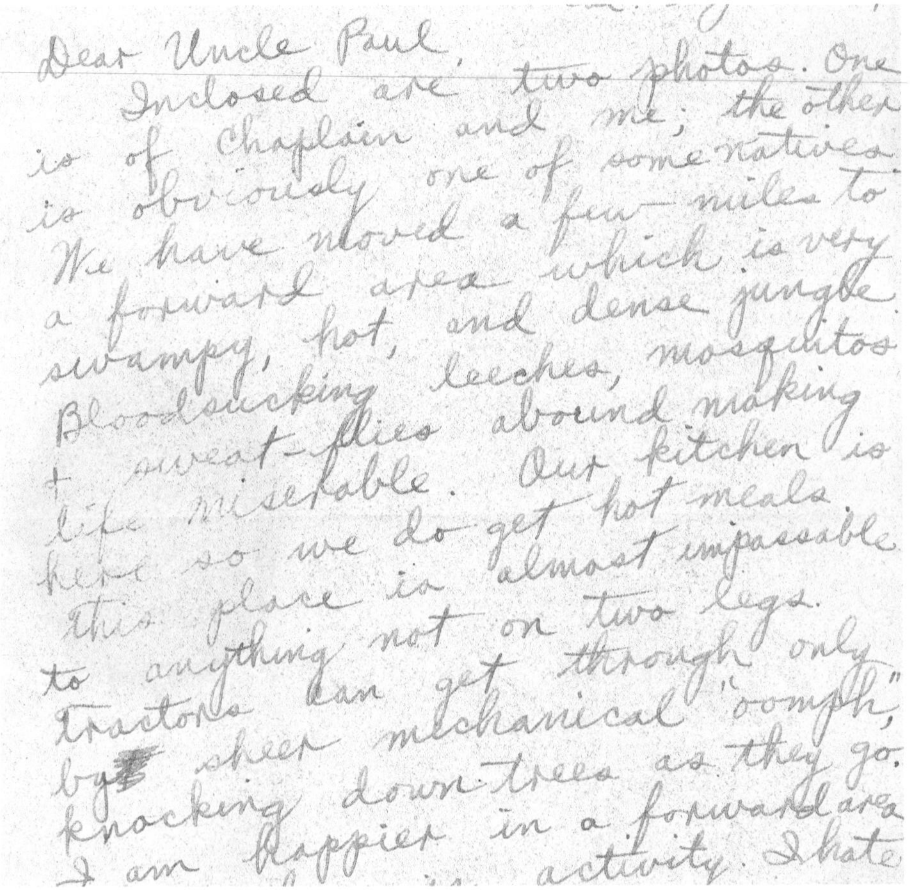

Sincerely, John [A. Martin]"

Dear Uncle Paul,
Thanks for sending the Christmas
greeting. That certainly is a cute
picture of Grand-dad and little
Robert Paul. Have been keeping
busy with instruction in weapons
firing, range construction. As
Munitions O. I get hooked on a lot
of odd jobs outside of my regular
job. I'm mess O. for H.Q. Co. and
agent finance O. Then I have a
platoon to look after. Inspections
take up a little time but allow
a plat. leader to find out exactly
what his men have. I believe in
periodic inspections. Mail censoring
kills more time especially in a rest
area where the men don't worry
about bullets and consequently write

Dear Uncle Paul,
Inclosed are two photos. One
is of Chaplain and me; the other
is obviously one of some natives.
We have moved a few miles to
a forward area which is very
swampy, hot, and dense jungle.
Bloodsucking leeches, mosquitos
+ sweat-flies abound making
life miserable. Our kitchen is
here so we do get hot meals
this place is almost impassable
to anything not on two legs.
Tractors can get through only
by sheer mechanical "oomph,"
knocking down trees as they go.
I am happier in a forward area
activity. I hate

"New Guinea
1 June '44

Dear Uncle Paul,

[Spelling is unaltered] Inclosed are two photos: One is of Chaplain and me; the other is obviously one of natives. We have moved a few miles to a forward area which is very swampy, hot, and dense jungle. Bloodsucking leeches, mosquitos & sweat-flies abound making life miserable. Our kitchen is here so we do get hot meals; this place is almost impassable to anything not on two legs. Tractors can get through only by sheer mechanical "oomph," knocking down trees as they go. I am happier in a forward area where there is activity. I hate to sit in a rear area and get the news second hand.

Being a newspaper man yourself you can appreciate how a story can get all screwed up & twisted after going from the original teller to the next hearers... No leaves in sight for us yet. How I'd like to let myself go for about 15 days in Sydney, Melbourne or Adelaide. Keep the news hot and we'll do our best to make it sizzling on this end. Sincerely,

John A. [Martin]"

Staff Sergeant Jessie Carrington McGhee from West Virginia served with the U.S. Army in the relentless island-hopping campaign across the Pacific, dying in the Philippines on October 22, 1944. In a letter home to his sister-in-law Garnette, he mentions taking part in the successful attack on Kwajalein Atoll at the beginning of February 1944. After five days of hard fighting, 41,000 American troops were landed and overcame stubborn Japanese resistance to capture the islands in the Atoll. Once the fighting was over, McGhee's unit was rotated back to Hawaii for rest and training.

"Sunday Night
Feb 27, 1944

Dear Garnette & all
[Spelling is unaltered] Will answer your letter after waiting so long. But you will haft to excuse me this time for I was tending a party with the Japs. I suppose you have read all about it Garnette. The battle of the Marshalls. Our out fit fought on Kurjakin Island in the Kwajalein atoll. I can say for sure now I killed one of those Japs. I am not abit ashame of it. I would love to get me a hell of a lot more. We are now safe back here in the Hawaiian Islands. And I'am sure glad to be back to. That Jungle fighting sure is tuff. I just wounder what they have in store for us Next. But all we can do is waite and traine untell our hearts pop out. No Garnette I haven't a girl friend over here. You are lucky to get to talk to one. Most of the girls here are Jap's and Chinese. There isn't to many American girls here. Any way my girl friends are those back there in the States. For our pass time here we get a few passes. We have free shoes here every Night. And

Above: A soldier protects his face from the incessant flies in the Western Desert, North Africa, as he writes a letter home.

some stage showes. We play a lot of sports all the time on Sunday like today we write letters, play cards or go some where to the show. Its Nothing like back in the States. . . Well Garnette I will close for now will write more Next time

Love to all
Jess"
[West Virginia Archive]

Paul Stephens served as a navy ensign as a pilot in the Pacific. He was killed in a plane crash only weeks before the surrender of Japan, and reprinted below is his last letter home and the standard cable (following page) received by families of a missing U.S. soldier or sailor.

"July 23, 1945

Dear Folks—I received some back letters a couple of days ago & I believe I have all the mail I was missing. However we haven't had any recent letters for several days & probably won't for a while longer.

It is a relief to be out of the heat—at last I feel rested after a few hours sleep and I do mean few. I am still well though & that's the big thing.

I think we are going to get some write ups after we get back home. I don't think they will be released before a war correspondence for the Sat. Ev. Post is aboard and collecting material about our squadron. It is a break for us to get the publicity. He is riding with me on all my hops which is a bigger break for me. You may have heard of him—Richard Tregaskis, author of "Guadalcanal Diary." He has covered all battle fronts since the war started. He was on the Hornet when Doolittle raid was launched for Japan, was in the Wasp when Torpedo Eight was practically wiped out, was in on the Italian front, Normandy beach-head & has flown with the B 24s. He is a swell fellow & we feel flattered to have him with us. So some day you may see my likeness on the Post along with an article on our squadron. Please don't say anything about this outside the family—I would rather nothing be said until if & when it is published."

July 23

Dear Folks -
I received some back letters a couple of days ago & I believe I have all the mail I was missing. However we haven't had any recent letters for several days & probably won't for a while longer.
It is a relief to be out of the heat - at last I feel rested after a few hours sleep and I do mean few. I am still well though & thats the big thing.
I think we are going to get some write ups after we get back home, I don't think they will be released before. a war correspondence for the Sat. Eve Post is aboard and collecting material about our squadron. It is a break for us to get the publicity. He is riding with me on all my hops which is a bigger break for me. You may have heard of him - Richard Tregaskis

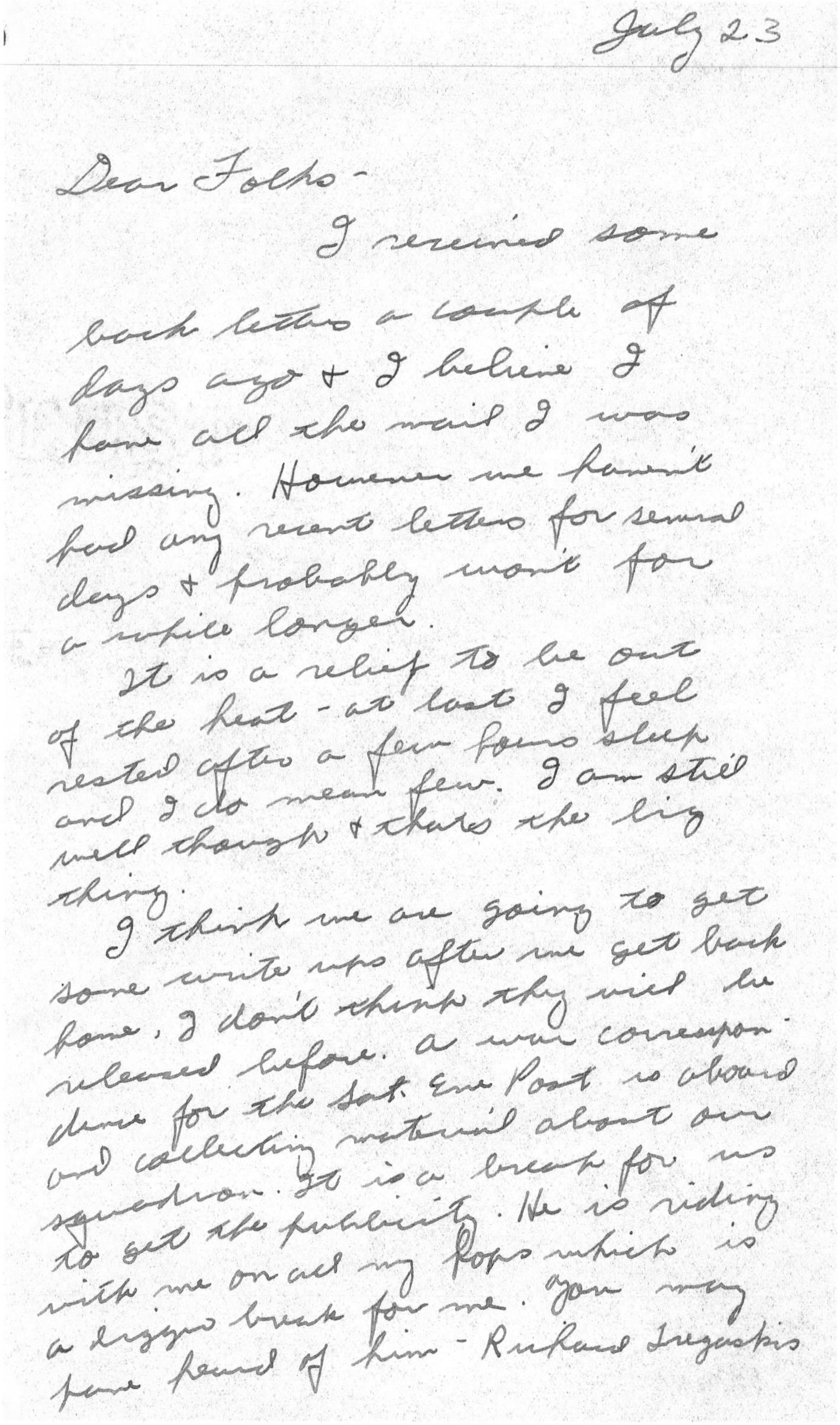

"WESTERN UNION

MR AND MRS HARRY TYLER STEPHENS 1945 AUG 8

I DEEPLY REGRET TO INFORM YOU THAT YOUR SON ENSIGN PAUL RAMSEY STEPHENS USNR HAS BEEN MISSING IN PLANE CRASH SINCE 28 JULY 1945 IN THE SERVICE OF HIS COUNTRY. YOUR GREAT ANXIETY IS APPRECIATED AND YOU WILL BE FURNISHED DETAILS WHEN RECEIVED. TO PREVENT POSSIBLE AID TO OUR ENEMIES PLEASE DO NOT DIVULGE THE NAME OF HIS SHIP OR STATION UNLESS THE GENERAL CIRCUMSTANCES ARE MADE PUBLIC IN NEWS STORIES

VICE ADMIRAL RANDALL JACOBS CHIEF OF NAVAL PERSONNEL"

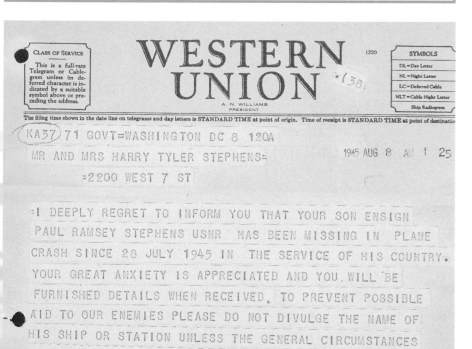

Such catastrophic news was often slightly offset by letters of condolence from comrades who explained to relatives exactly what had happened to their loved ones, and went some way toward explaining how they died, if not why. Buell F. Payne, a Flight Officer in the U.S. Navy was reported missing on September 6, 1943, after a mission in the South Pacific. This letter, to his parents from one of his colleagues, explains the circumstances surrounding his death.

"My Dear Mrs. Payne,

I am writing this letter at the request of Lieutenant Colonel Woodrow B. Wilmot my commanding officer, as I was on the flight from which your son is reported missing.

"Boo" that is what we called him, was flying on my wing. We took off about 10:30 on September 6th and flew about 160 miles where we rendezvoused with the bombers of the flight. From there we went on to our combat mission, and just as it was completed we were jumped by Japanese planes. We were outnumbered about 4 to 1. and became split up during the ensuing fight. I saw Boo several times during the fight, and he was making a good accounting of himself. My plane became badly shot up, one gasoline tank destroyed and I had to make a run for the nearest field with a Jap plane on my tail. No one saw Boo go down, but as he did not return to his home field, he was reported missing in action.

Boo's loss is a great one to both his squadron and to myself. We went clear through pre-flight and flying school together and were very close friends.

Sincerely John R. Workman"
[Taken from *Corson County News*, December 2, 1943]

By 1942, Germany was involved in a war on two fronts. Operation Barbarossa, launched in the summer of 1941 had not been the lightning invasion the Germans had hoped for. Despite the superiority of their equipment and well-trained troops, they were arrested by the rigors of the Russian winter and by the sheer numbers of soldiers that the Russians could muster in defense of their motherland. Nevertheless, with Stalingrad (now Volgograd) and Moscow threatened, Stalin was worried, and at the Moscow Conference in August 1942 with Churchill and Roosevelt's representative,

Averell Harriman, urged the U.S. and Great Britain to launch a second front. Churchill declined on behalf of Britain and the U.S.A., but in this letter to Roosevelt, Stalin tried to drive a wedge between them by implying that it was Churchill's decision alone.

As the result of an exchange of views in Moscow which took place on August 12th of this year, I ascertained that the Prime Minister of Great Britain, Mr. Churchill, considered the organisation of a second front in Europe in 1942 to be impossible.

As is well known, the organisation of a second front in Europe in 1942 was pre-decided during the sojourn of Molotov in London and it found expression in the agreed Anglo-Soviet communiqué published on June 12th last.

It is also known that the organisation of a second front in Europe had as its object the withdrawal of Germany forces from the Eastern front to the West, and the creation in the West of a serious base of resistance to the German-Fascist forces and the affording of relief by this means to the situation of the Soviet forces on the Soviet-German front in 1942.

It will be easily understood that the Soviet Command built their plan of summer and autumn operations calculating on the creation of a second front in Europe in 1942.

It is easy to grasp that the refusal of the Government of Great Britain to create a second front in 1942 in Europe inflicts a moral blow to the whole of Soviet public opinion, which calculates on the creation of a second front, and that it complicates the situation of the Red Army at the front and prejudices the plan of the Soviet Command.

I am not referring to the fact that the difficulties arising for the Red Army as the result of the refusal to create a second front in 1942 will undoubtedly have to deteriorate the military situation of England and all the remaining allies.

It appears to me and my colleagues that the most favourable conditions exist in 1942 for the creation of a second front in Europe, inasmuch as almost all the forces of the Germany army, and the best forces to boot have been withdrawn to the Eastern front,

"As a result of the exchange of views in Moscow which took place on August 18th of this year, I ascertained that the Prime Minister of Great Britain, Mr Churchill considered the organisation of a second front in Europe in 1942 to be impossible.

As is well known, the organisation of a Second Front in Europe in 1942 was pre-decided during the sojourn of Molotov in London and it found expression in the agreed Anglo-Soviet communiqué published in June 12th last.

It is known that the organisation of a Second Front in Europe had as its objective the withdrawal of German forces from the Eastern Front to the West, and the creation in the West of a serious base of resistance to the German-fascist forces and the affording of relief by this means to the situation of the Soviet forces on the Soviet-German frontier in 1942.

It will be easily understood that the Soviet Command built their plan of summer and autumn operations calculating upon the creation of a second front in 1942.

It is easy to grasp that the refusal of the government of Great Britain to create a Second Front in 1942 in Europe inflicts a moral blow to the whole of Soviet public opinion, which calculates on the creation of a second front, and that it complicates the situation of the Red Army at the front and prejudices the plans of the Soviet Command...

It appears to me and my colleagues that the most favourable conditions exist in 1942 for the creation of a second front in Europe, inasmuch as almost all the forces of the German army, and the best forces to boot, have been withdrawn to the Eastern Front, leaving in Europe an inconsiderable amount of forces and these of inferior quality. It is unknown whether the year of 1943 will offer conditions for the creation of a second front as favourable as 1942. We are of the opinion, therefore, that it is particularly in 1942 that the creation of a second front in Europe is possible and should be effected. I was however unfortunately unsuccessful in convincing Mr Prime Minister of Great Britain hereof, while Mr Harriman, the representative of the President of the U.S.A. fully supported Mr Prime Minister in the negotiations held in Moscow.

J Stalin
August 13 1942."

The Eastern Front was one of the most bitterly fought campaigns of the war, with both sides guilty of unspeakable atrocities. This desperate letter, written by an anonymous German officer after the retreat from Stalingrad offers a rare insight into the feelings of an average German soldier.

"I might have been killed three times by now, but it would have always have been suddenly, without my being prepared. Now things are different; since this morning I know how things stand; and since I feel freer this way, I want you also to be free from apprehension and uncertainty.

I was shocked when I saw the map. We are entirely alone, without help from the outside. Hitler has left us in the lurch. If the airfield is still in our possession, this letter may still get out. Our position is to the north of the city. The men of my battery have some inkling of it, too, but they don't know it as clearly as I do. So this is what the end looks like. Hannes and I will not surrender; yesterday, after our infantry had retaken a position, I saw four men who had been taken prisoner by the Russians. No, we shall not go into captivity. When Stalingrad has fallen, you'll know that I shall not come back.

You are the wife of a German officer; so you will take what I have to tell you, upright and unflinching, as upright as you stood on the station platform the day I left you for the East. I am no letter-writer and my letters have never been longer than a page. Today there would be a great deal to say, but I will save it for later, i.e., six weeks if all goes well and a hundred years if it doesn't. You will have to reckon with the latter possibility. If all goes well, we shall be able to talk about it for a long time, so why should I attempt to write much now, since it comes hard to me. If things turn out badly, words won't do much good anyhow."

Above: The battered city of Stalingrad undergoes artillery fire during its siege by German forces in 1942 and 1943.

Below: Soviet forces eventually won this important battle when German forces attacked Stalingrad.

British and American planners realized that years of work and training were needed before a second front could succeed. U.S. troops were shipped to Britain throughout 1942–1944 to prepare for the largest amphibious invasion in history, and joined British, Canadian, French, and Polish forces. The Supreme Commander, Dwight D. Eisenhower, sent this uplifting message to the troops of the Allied Expeditionary Forces on June 6, 1944, as Order of the Day, on the morning of D-Day, the invasion of Normandy.

Above and right: American troops invaded mainland Europe on June 6, 1944, and later wrote home about their experiences.

"Soldiers, Sailors and Airmen of the Allied Expeditionary Forces: You are about to embark upon the Great Crusade, toward which we have striven these many months. The eyes of the world are upon you. The hopes and prayers of liberty-loving people everywhere march with you. In company with our brave Allies and brothers-in-arms on other Fronts you will bring about the destruction of the German war machine, the elimination of Nazi tyranny over oppressed peoples of Europe, and security for ourselves in a free world.

Your task will not be an easy one. Your enemy is well trained, well equipped and battle-hardened. He will fight savagely.

But this is the year 1944! Much has happened since the Nazi triumphs of 1940–41. The United Nations have inflicted upon the Germans great defeats, in open battle, man-to-man. Our air offensive has seriously reduced their strength in the air and their capacity to wage war on the ground. Our Home Fronts have given us an over-whelming superiority in weapons and munitions of war, and placed at our disposal great reserves of trained fighting men. The tide has turned! The free men of the world are marching together to Victory!

I have full confidence in your courage, devotion to duty and skill in battle. We will accept nothing less than full victory!

Good Luck! And let us all beseech the blessing of Almighty God upon this great and noble undertaking."

John Farley was an American artillery officer who left behind an English fiancée in the WRENS. After a whirlwind romance, he wrote witty, lovesick, and illuminating letters to her, describing a little of the fighting in Normandy in 1944.

Above: The beaches of Normandy, June 1944.

"Monday 17:44, 0910 hrs, CP Command Post

My beloved Pat:
Cet lettre est ecrit sur le papier que nous avons pris des Boches. Pas mal, n'est-ce pas? But it's got me woozy trying to space the letters properly. The above French is a sample of what my French conversation sounds like. As you can readily see, if I am to do any good with the girls at Juan-les-Pins, as you once suggested, my French will have to improve but greatly. No mail from you since the 7th at this writing, although I have a feeling that at least four will be in the evening sack. Hope so anyhow.

After moving into our marshalling area—that's where the troops wait and prepare for the ferry ride cross the Channel—the plan for the invasion began to shape up. Phase one was our fond farewell to home station. All communication had been frozen from about the time you received my last telegram. We broke camp in the dead of night. My unit was considerably broken up. Much to my dismay I was to be separated from my great and good friend, Charles, as well as my captain. Rather somber for all of us—this farewell—as it was made quite plain to us that the next time we would see each other would be—you guessed it Somewhere in France—unless!

Our battalion, dear little lady, is a crack outfit. My battery, naturally, the best. And as was fitting, it got a particularly hazardous job in the initial stages of the assault. Only a well-trained and well disciplined outfit could do the job. As my job is not so vitally tied up with actual firing—I'm more of a firing data preparation "expert", I was excluded from this party. However I did go along with the advance elements and had all things gone exactly as planned your boy would have hit the beach right behind the infantry. As it was, we were forced to wait in the channel a day or so until the situation warranted landing.

The landing went off without a hitch. The giant LST was going hell bent for election at about 5 mph to previously selected positions. The beach really was that crowded.

I must regretfully report that there were evidences of a great and bloody struggle at the spot where we landed. All day previous we had lain offshore and watched the operations through glasses. Sort of like grandstand seats at the biggest show on earth. Only the price of admission ran sort of high.

The beach was cluttered with abandoned military debris. But for every piece of equipment that had fallen because of the Boche's defenses or fire, it seemed as though three had gotten ashore and been set up for business. It seemed so damn funny. There were more bulldozers and road making equipment ashore than shooting pieces. All these construction engineers working with the aplomb of a chain gang. What a place for a strike, I thought.

Did not stay on the beach too long. Following a strict path through the mine fields of course, my gang—survey and communications soldiers—soon contacted a battery messenger who guided us to our position. Before arriving I ran into a schoolmate that I had been trying to contact all the time I was in England.

Upon arriving at the battery position, great cries of reunion. Then plenty of work. The battery had been getting some good licks in the night before but the conditions under which we had been forced to set up shop were so dangerous that all efforts were being made to effect a displacement. I'll stop for now. I'll leave out the usual words of endearment and great passion so you can send this letter to my folks.

All my love,
John"

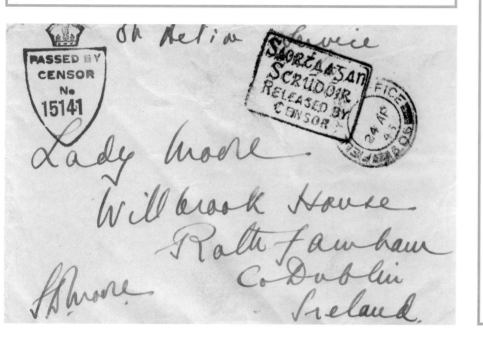

By September 1944, Bob Hoesley had fought across France from Normandy toward the Ardennes.

"Dear Frank,

Its about time I reported in again I guess. A lot of things have happened and are happening since I wrote the last time. We've been here in France for sometime and although I like the country and ways here better than in England I still repeat—"there is no place like America." I'm sure that goes for every G.I. here.

It might not be so long now though and I'm planning on buying a South Dakota fishing license early next spring.

A lot of boys like Ernie Utter and Hank Trager would certainly be familiar with some of the spots we're going through now. We're not permitted to mention towns we hit, but we've made a long trip from where we first hit France. I haven't been in "Gay Parie" yet but we were close and then went the other way. Maybe I'll make it after the war, but about all I'm interested in then is to get home.

Due to the liquor shortage there at home here's something that might interest you. We found a German wine cellar containing 3500 cases of red wine and cognac. Personally I don't care if we find any more. There's a lot of headaches in a couple of those bottles.

The Heinies are running so fast sometimes, that we're picking up a lot of good equipment intact.

Today every soldier you see has a fur jacket. The result of a train captured, headed for the Russian front.

I got a kick out of the article you put in the paper about the arrival of my baby girl. Didn't I say things have happened since I wrote last.

If I can make it I'll send dad a bottle of cognac for you and him to get a headache.

Best Regards,

Bob Hoesley"

[Taken from *Corson County News*, September 28, 1944]

Right: American soldiers eat
Christmas dinner in An Song, Korea.

Far right: A grief-stricken American
infantryman, whose buddy has been
killed in action, is comforted by
another soldier.

Wars of the Late Twentieth Century and Beyond

The Cold War, which dominated international politics from 1946 until 1991, was something of a misnomer; although the superpowers, the U.S.A. and U.S.S.R., did not fight each other head on, their deep suspicion and mutual mistrust meant that satellite states erupted into conflict many times. The U.S. involvement in both Korea and Vietnam was a reaction to the threat of communism spreading throughout Southeast Asia, and the forces of North Vietnam were financed and equipped by the U.S.S.R. and China.

Korea 1950–1953

A mere five years after the end of World War II, America and Britain found themselves embroiled in Korea in a war which began as a post-colonial struggle and became an international conflict in June 1950. In 1945, the U.S.A. and U.S.S.R. administered the surrender of the Japanese forces which had occupied Korea: the U.S.S.R. dealt with those north of the 38th parallel, and the U.S.A. those south of that line. Having established a commission to form a provisional government, the U.S.A. and U.S.S.R. soon disagreed over the legitimacy of the various political groups competing to rule the country and in 1947 the U.S.A. asked the United Nations to unify the country. By 1950, the arbitrary border of the 38th parallel had become an international frontier dividing Kim Il Sung's Democratic People's Republic of Korea in the north from Syngman Rhee's Republic of Korea in the south. Recurrent border clashes developed into war when North Korea invaded the south, and the U.S. believed that the U.S.S.R. had orchestrated the whole affair.

The U.S.A. and South Korea led 17 combatant nations, including Great Britain, Australia, Canada, and Turkey, defending South Korea against the communist forces of the north. The invasion by the North Korean People's Army (N.K.P.A.) swept right through South Korea as far south as the Taegu-Pusan perimeter and destroyed half of the Republic of Korea's (R.O.K.)

army. Surprised by the intervention of American air, naval, and ground forces, by August 1950 the N.K.P.A. found themselves stranded at the end of an overextended supply line. Led initially by Douglas MacArthur and later by Matthew B. Ridgway, American troops fought a bitterly-contested war against the Chinese-and Soviet-backed North Koreans. Truce talks began in October 1951, but communist guerrillas continued to harass the south even beyond the official armistice in July 1953.

Gen. Lewis B. "Chesty" Puller, a veteran marine commander, wrote surprisingly tender letters to his wife after the retreat from Chosin, Korea, 1950. He had landed at Inchon with MacArthur and the 1st Marine Corps in September 1950.

"December 9, 1950

Darling:
I understand that the news back home is to the effect that the First Marine Division is cut off, surrounded by the Chinese, etc. etc... God is helping us; so do not worry, Virginia. I am confident that I will get back home to come for you, Virginia Mc, Martha Leigh and little Lewis. Believe me! My love for you will last forever, Virginia, even into the next life and then on. The hardest thing that I have ever done was to tell you goodbye.

As always your loving husband"

John Rademacher fought with the Marines and penned lively descriptive letters to his family.

"South Bank Han River
April 4th 1951

Hello Dear People,
Received packages last week. Really hit the spot. We were up on ground where we didn't get chow and down they drop our mail with the packages, two from you and some Easter candy from Jean. The guys in my fire team reluctantly helped me eat it up. We share everything, even the mud.

Moved up along the Hoensong road N.W. until we hit the end of it. Then we crossed about six miles of mountainous country carrying all our gear and ammunition. We were like pack mules for a few days. When we got back, we found out we were moving out in two days.

No chow yesterday or the day before as we were too far from our supply route. Got some rice and dried corn and tried to make a meal. The rice fills the empty beer pit. We boiled the dry corn all day and finally chewed it of the cob, but the flavor was kinda like leather. Rations came in today and they really tasted first class.

There's a lot of artillery fire but all they are doing is knocking off mountain tops. The Gooks seem to all have taken off. Bunch of fellows got relieved from here yesterday. New replacements are coming up. Tell brother David Noel not to jump into this party.

Must move now,
Son John

P.S. Hello again,
We have secured the north bank of the Han river where we were relieved by the 23rd Inf. We had only two fellows killed in two weeks. We fought on the high ground. 35 minutes after the army relieved us, they had eleven casualties. They use the road to march up... we use the bushes and ditches.

Now we are set up in the flat just south of Seoul. McCrary of Green Bay, I knew him well, got hit by schrapnel, but guess he will be okay.

Looks like we will sit around for a few weeks and probably be pulled out.

Robert Frances would have enjoyed the landing we made on the river. We used duck boats. One got stuck in the mud. The gooks tried to hit it with mortar but missed. A hill went up directly from shore like Iwo. Were corsairs diving a couple yards overhead. When they'd let up the artillery took over with white phosphorus and H.E... more fun.

Johnny"

In the following letter, Johnny mentions helicopters, which were first used seriously in combat during this war and revolutionized methods of resupply and troop deployment.

"Sept. 25, 1951

Hello All,

Am still horsing around, eating, sleeping, standing watches, working and the like.

One of those new copters they have just landed over by the C.P.. Guess they can carry about 15 men. Marines have about 20 of em up here, use em for supply and evacuation. Only been over here for a few weeks.

Our Co. is supposed to get some kind of commendation for taking a hill about a week ago that 2 or 3 other outfits couldn't take. We moved around them at nite and hit em from the rear. Are now in the rear recouperating again.

Word has it that we won't be committed to assault anymore as they figure they have the lines straight. Must be sumpin' in those new peace talks. The gooks can't be stalling any more. They threw the rest of their troops at us so can't be stalling much more.

They sent a few against us back there but were met with 60mm 81mm 42 mm mortars, 4.5 rockets, 105mm 155mm & 16in artillery and didn't get too far. Guess the fighting is about over in this sector.

Have been doing a lot of scrounging (picking up chow) around the area. Have it made when friends are on guard. The chow they're feeding isn't to bad but as you'd say, kinda skoskhi.

So Long,

John J."

Right: Men of Company A, 1st Battalion, 19th Infantry Regiment, 24th U.S. Division, receive their New Year's Day dinner in 1952.

Vietnam 1965–1975

No nation is left unscarred by a war, but the Vietnam conflict had (and still has) an all-pervasive effect on America. U.S. participation in the war was a highly controversial issue both domestically and internationally, and the nation was splintered: some supported the war; others opposed it; another group opposed it, but its members were drafted to fight anyway. Furthermore, America did not emerge as the victor and after the long years of fighting many people questioned the rationale behind U.S. involvement. This attitude was reflected in the treatment of the returning troops, brave men who had served their country and whose actions did not receive the acknowledgment that was their due. It was not until 1982, seven years after the last choppers had lifted off from the besieged embassy in Saigon, that America acknowledged its debt to the 58,000 fallen and erected a war memorial in Washington.

The U.S.A.'s involvement in Vietnam was gradual, almost secretive, and began in the 1950s as Vietnam suffered its own post-colonial crisis between nationalist and communist forces. The Kennedy administration sent soldiers, but referred to them as "advisers" to train the South Vietnamese in counter-insurgency techniques to tackle the communist Viet Minh. U.S. combat troops were committed in 1965 after North Vietnamese attacks on U.S. bases, notoriously the Gulf of Tonkin incident in August 1964.

The U.S.A. sent increasingly large numbers of troops, who encountered deadly and effective guerrilla tactics on the part of the Viet Cong, soldiers who were fighting in their own terrain and seemed to melt away into the jungle. More than one writer mentions the problems of trying to fire on an almost invisible enemy. The Tet Offensive of 1968, a coordinated series of attacks on both major cities and rural targets, was an attempt by the north to destabilize the Saigon regime once and for all, and to force the U.S.A. to withdraw its forces. After an initial hint of success, it failed, and the Viet Cong suffered serious casualties. At the same time, however, the U.S. public began to question their country's involvement in the war and President Johnson began moves to lessen the U.S. military commitment and to bring about peace negotiations. The complicated process of withdrawing troops, while at the same time maintaining the viability of the South Vietnamese regime in Saigon continued under President Nixon, who also launched strikes into Viet Cong safe havens in Laos and Cambodia.

Right: Soldiers of the 2nd Battalion, 4th Marine Regiment, at Fire Support Base Russell, take a break from their work to pick up their mail.

A peace agreement was finally signed in Paris in January 1973, but fighting broke out again in 1974. By then, the United States was engrossed with its own internal problems, so North Vietnamese troops took advantage of American preoccupation to invade South Vietnam, capturing Saigon on April 30, 1975.

Robert Feighny was an army doctor who was sent to Vietnam in 1964 as an "adviser," part of the force which was intended to train the South Vietnamese to support themselves. His letters mention the scope of his activities, tending both civilians and soldiers.

"Nha Tiang
My future home
23 April [1964]

My darling wife and children,
I arrived in Nha Tiang with some Santa Barbara lemons, potatoes, dehydrated granoles and a few barrels of gasoline. This place seems to be about the end of the line... There is a great deal of orthopedic work that can be done in this area especially among civilian people. There is the American army and air force in this area however there is very little if any war activity in this section of the country. We have a few Americans that work with the native people in this area...

Another source of some patients is from the medical missionary who has a small hospital and his patients may get x-rays here and we treat a few of these people in our hospital. However we are not to have more than a very small number. Then there is the Army of Vietnam's hospital that handles the soldiers who are injured. They like to have some assistance... It is impossible to solve all the problems.

Living conditions are extremely difficult with so much poverty and a life has such little value over here. This is a different part of the world. Americans are so well off and have such a great form of life and luxuries.

I am living in a grass hut—I'll send you a picture of it soon. The John is across the street, the shower is the next building over. We are fortunate in that we have running water (cold). My little cot has a mosquito net, malaria tablets. Scotch is very cheap! The food is all right... I think you are better off living in our nice home. Things will be better next year—I'm paying off my debt for being an American and in the army.

#5

Nha Tiang
My Future Home
23 April
Letter 5.

My darling wife and children,
I arrived in Nha Tiang with some Santa Barbara lemons, potatoes, dehydrated, granoles, and a few barrels of gasoline. This place seems to be about the end of the line. Lydell Wright was extremely glad to see me and others have been very nice. There is a great deal of orthopedic work that can be done in this area especially among the civilian people. There is the American army and air force in this area however there is very little if any war activity in this section of the country. We have a few Americans that work with the native

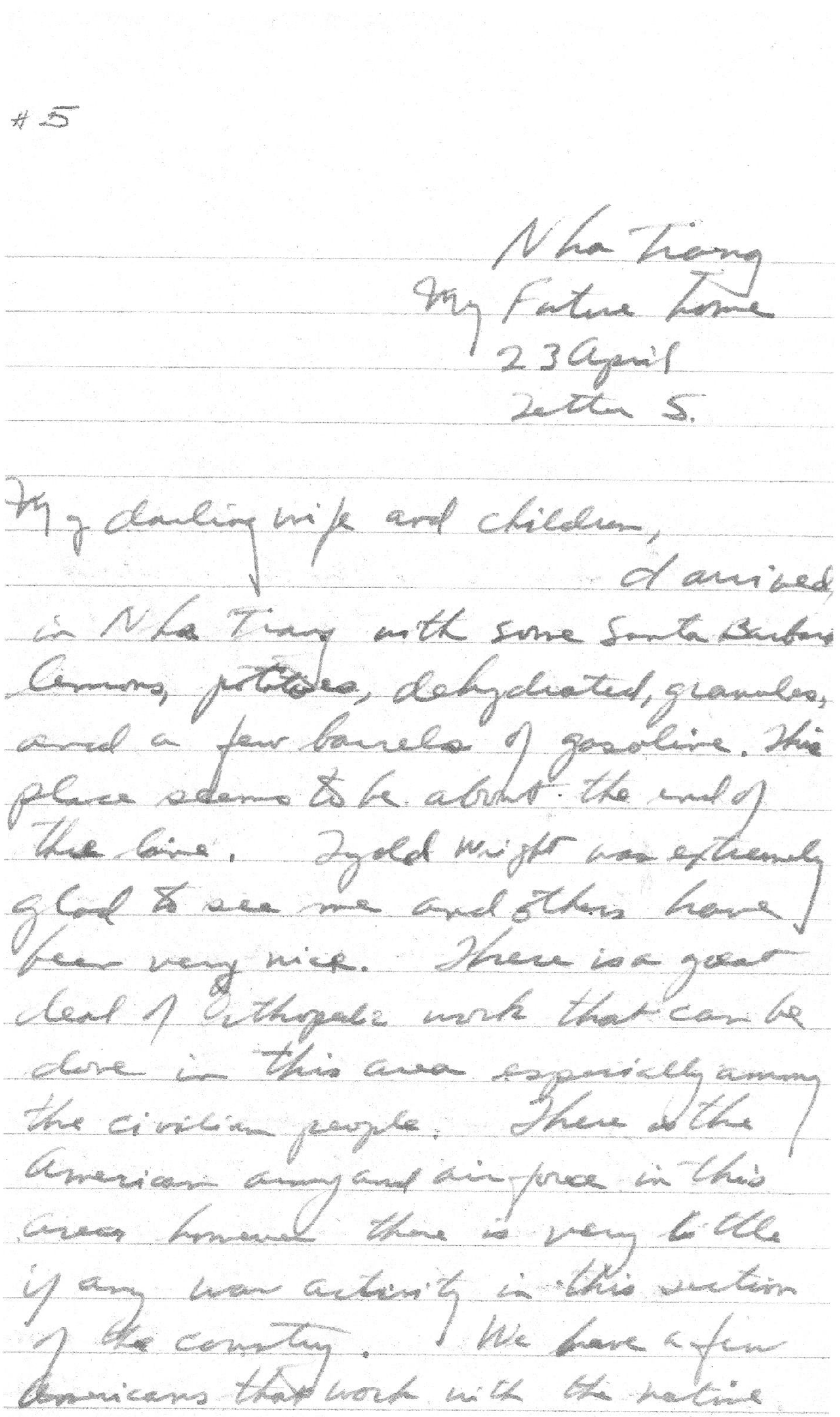

Above: A group of marines pause for a cigarette after securing a battle-scarred building in Hue.

In a few more days I should receive some mail from you to give some sunshine and happiness in my life. I love you and take good care of yourself and the children. With all my love, your loving husband,

Bob"

A regular soldier, Stan Hominski had enlisted in the army in 1964, and married shortly before he was sent to Vietnam in 1968. He served with the B Troop, 3/4 Cavalry, 25th Infantry Division. His letter expresses the very common feeling of guilt that he could have acted more quickly to save a comrade.

"25 May, 1968

Dear Roberta,

Today is probably the worst day I have ever lived in my entire, short life. Once again we were in contact with Charlie, and once again we suffered losses. The losses we had today hit home, as my best friend in this shit hole was killed. He was only 22 years old and was going on R&R on the first of June to meet his wife in Hawaii. I feel that if I was only a half second sooner in pulling the trigger, he would still be alive.

Strange how short a time a half of a second is—the difference between life and death. This morning we were talking about how we were only two years different in age and how we both had gotten married before coming to this place. You know, I can still feel his presence as I write this letter and hope that I am able to survive and leave this far behind me.

If there is a place called Hell this surely must be it, and we must be the Devil's disciples doing all his dirty work. I keep asking myself if there is a God, then how the hell come young men with so much to live for have to die. I just hope that his death is not in vain.

I look forward to the day when I will take my R&R. If I play my cards right, I should be able to get it for Hawaii so our anniversary will be in that time frame. The reason I say this is by Sept., I will have more than enough time in country to get my pick of places and dates. I promise I will do everything necessary to insure that I make that date, and I hope that tomorrow is quiet.

We will be going into base camp soon for our three-day stand down. I will try to write you a longer letter at that time. Please don't worry too much about me, as if you won't, for I will take care of myself and look forward to the day I am able to be with you again.

Love,
Stan"

Massachusetts teenager Paul O'Connell was in Mike Company, 3rd Battalion, 5th Marine Corps. He enlisted at the age of 17 in 1968, trained as a rifleman and arrived in Vietnam in October 1968, where his unit operated out of the An Hoa base. O'Connell's letters display an incredible amount of bravado that hid what he now admits was pure terror. In one letter he describes air strikes exploding 1,000 yards away as "pretty cool to watch"; reading his letters, his parents must have worried beyond belief. In another letter, written near Christmas 1968, he asks his folks to send him a bottle of vodka, prefacing his request with "I'm gonna ask you to send me something, and I don't want ya to be surprised as I'm pretty well grown-up now. You've got to be over here." O'Connell epitomized the soldier who was little more than a child; he was old enough to fight and die for his country, but too young to buy a drink.

"23 May 69

Dear family!!!

Well, as I write you, I find myself in the same compound I was in the night before we left for Hill 500 and Operation Taylor Common. That was back on around December 8th.

This time, we are going on an operation to three different areas around the southern part of Da Nang. The three areas are Dodge City, Go Noi Island, and the Arizona Territory. Right now, they are said to be the hottest combat zones in Vietnam. So I hope God will be with me. So far, I've had good luck; but I'm starting to get scared

with only about 5 months left before I come home. I'll be lucky if I don't get hit again. But if I do, don't worry as the Marines and Navy take good care of us wounded.

I see Mama got a telephone call from Sharon the other day. Well, the reason I left her is because she's been going out with some guy by the name of Keith. Plus, the last time she wrote, she told me, quote, 'It's been so beautiful out, I haven't had time to write.'

She always adds a remark like this, and it makes me mad and gives me the impression I'm just being a fool keeping her. So, if she calls again, tell her to go to hell and not to wait for any letters from me because there's no way in the world I'll write her. But like I said, me and this girl from New York are getting pretty close.

Well, got to go for now. I'll write tomorrow; and, if Sharon calls again, tell her not to bother calling anymore. And, if you don't, I'll write and tell her myself.

Love, Paul

P.S. Have Marsha send me a picture, as there's a buddy of mine who wants to write her. Okay?"

Above: Three troopers sit out a downpour in the Demilitarized Zone.

133

O'Connell's unit was continuously in the thick of fighting for many months, as the Viet Cong attacked An Hua. He and his comrades lived on their nerves in miserable conditions, existing with little sleep, perpetually wet from the tropical rain and humid atmosphere, and scared witless by the presence of a terrorist enemy that shimmered almost invisibly around them until their presence was felt all too explosively.

"05 June 69

Dear Mom, Dad, Tommy and Marsha,

Received 2 letters from you on the 30th and 31st of May. Well, it sounds like summer has come to Quincy, finally. In a way I'd like to see a little bit of snow. Today wasn't too bad, it was only 102.

Well, we are still sitting on the river waiting for gooks. Today we killed an NVA officer and a NVA girl. They were in the act of, "you know what;" but, after you see your buddies killed, you get revenge anyway we can.

We also burned a village down and killed about 20 pigs. Plus, somehow, a little kid got in the way of a round. Tough shit!

I just wrote Cheryl and Bobby. Plus I got a letter from Paul Diaz and told him he could come up and see you people and maybe you could show him some of my pictures. Okay?

Let me tell you about my other girl. She's from the Bronx in New York and works for TWA Airlines. She's a ticket agent and has blond hair, 5'3", and blue eyes. She's out of this world and is something Daddy, Grandpa, Gus, and Arthur would whistle at as she went by, like they use to do when Annie walked by on Utica Street. Oh, her name is Lynn White. When I come home, she's going to fly up to see me, and I'll probably fly down to New York while I'm on leave.

Well got to go for now, but will write later.

Love you all, Paul"

Right: A patrol fords a small stream in the A Shau Valley.

This is an extraordinary letter which veers from boasting about killing a small child to enquiring after his family and chatting about a girlfriend. It is the letter of a man driven half mad by war. Thirty years later, O'Connell wrote "As for the small child, again, I heard about it secondhand; but I remember when I did, it didn't phase me at all. By now, I didn't care if we killed all the Vietnamese. It would have been easier than trying to sort which ones we were suppose to be helping, which ones were on our side, from the ones that were trying to kill me. They all looked alike with their devious smiles... I was slowly going crazy." About a month later O'Connell was hospitalized suffering from combat fatigue, but after a couple of weeks was sent back to his unit. As he now remarks, post-traumatic stress disorder was not a recognized medical condition during the Vietnam War.

Corporal Michael Alan McAninch, was a 22-year-old college student from Houston, Texas, when he joined the Marines. He wrote lyrical letters to his family, describing the Vietnamese landscape without displaying any rancor against the Vietnamese people. He was simply serving his country, but, like most of his comrades, counted the days until he was due home. He arrived at Da Nang in February 1969, where his unit, the 3rd Battalion, 1st Marine Division, was taking part in the Tet Counter Offensive.

"Sat., April 12, 1969
8:30am

Hello, Folks,
It's been a long time since I've written. I hope you will understand. We've been on an operation since March 29th, so this makes the 14th day out. It's called Operation Oklahoma Hills. We've had practically no time at all to write, and I was able, only yesterday, to send Joanie a second letter since being on the operation. It's a large-scale operation involving 7 battalions, all working in the mountains to the West and Southwest of Hill 10 where Mike Company is. We are now on Hill 1235—1235 feet above sea level, and it has really been rough, with about 50lbs of gear on our backs, going up and down the mountains to get to the next higher mountain. Well at least we are at our final objective now and will stay here two more days before heading back to the hill to arrive there about the 28th or 29th—a whole month in the mountains. The first week was real hot and climbing got difficult—we had a few heat casualties but I kept taking my salt tablets and conserved my water so I escaped that ordeal.

So far we've been really lucky—we've encountered very few of the enemy and our platoon hasn't even seen one since the beginning of the op'. Hope it stays that way. I've lost about 10 or 15 pounds but still feel pretty good although kind of hungry right now. The last week has been pretty bad as far as supplies of food and water getting to us. We are so far up that clouds and fog prevent the re-supply choppers from getting to us, so we've been going on maybe 1 or 2 meals a day and 3 canteens of water.

We've really been going through some beautiful mountain terrain, though, with moist rain forests and cold mountain streams tumbling over large boulders—really quite a sight. It reminds me of the trip we took to Ridgecrest in So. Carolina when I was 14. But not much time to stop, relax, and appreciate the view. If the day is clear we can see the ocean and barely make out DaNang in the distance about 20 miles away to the N.E.

Yesterday was a great day; I got 2 letters from Joanie my first 2 days out but no mail since then. Then yesterday—WOW—8 letters I think it was—3 from Joanie, 1 from Mother, 1 from Dad, 1 from Mary Ann, and 1 from Aunt Lois and Uncle Leslie, and the newsletter from RPBC. It was great—we got chow and I ate and settled back for a few minutes with a can of hot cocoa and a Marlboro to read the letters. It couldn't have been a better day. I was so hungry for letters and 8 at one time was almost too much...

I think about you all, all the time. Spring back in Houston, really sounds great. Joanie writes and describes the beautiful day, and you tell me about the yellow flowers and newly planted rose bushes. It sure will be good to get back to the Hill and take a shower and partake of all the necessities that seem like luxuries out here.

You asked if there was anything you could send me—YES—would you believe this list. Really, you know we think of things that we would like to get, like kool-aid for our water and homemade cookies, etc., but now when we are all so hungry our minds start thinking of food. I thought that I'd make a list of some things you could send me. The more I thought, the more I realized that there are so many things that are right there in the supermarket that cost very little but to me here would seem like a feast and I would go wild over...

[What follows is a touching multi-page wish-list to combat the infamous blandness of C-Rations, including the following: Mom's homemade cookies, onion bread, biscuits, cakes, etc.; Nestle's Quik;

135

Ritz Crackers and cheese; Chef-Boy-Ar-Dee Dinners; all kinds of breads; donuts; instant oatmeal; Lipton's soups; marshmallows; cocoa etc.]

Well, I've talked mostly about food, but I still think of you very much and love you all dearly. I constantly think how great it will be to get back to Houston and you and Joanie.

I'll close for now.

Your loving and well son,
Michael"

Having succumbed to malaria and enjoyed convalescence away from the firing line, Michael was sent back to his battalion in time for the summer offensive of 1969. Less than three weeks after writing this letter he was killed by mortar fire while defending his squad from a Viet Cong attack. His selfless and heroic actions earned him a posthumous Bronze Star.

"Sunday, August 10, 1969 10:20am

Dear Mother, Dad, Pat & Mary Ann,

Right now we are in a village west of Hill 55 for the day. I'm writing on a table that the Vietnamese build themselves out of bamboo. It's strange—they have tables and benches, etc. out here, the things we would like but don't have up on the Hill.

Sometime between the 15th and 20th of this month, the 7th Marine Regiment will be moving. We haven't gotten any specific word yet, but the word seems to be that we will be going South to set up somewhere around Chu Lai. Other than that I don't know. How long we will be there and exactly where I don't know either. Just have to wait for further word...

I'm hoping that if I have to stay over here the whole 13 months, that I'll be able to make Sgt. The reason I say "13 months" is that

Above: A mortar crew at Khe Sahn spend many long, noisy hours behind sandbag defenses.

we are all hoping to be among those being pulled out of Vietnam. I read the other day that another 100,000 military personnel were to be removed sometime soon. We are hoping that the 7th Marines will be next to be pulled out because, as we understand it, the 7th is now the senior division after the 9th Marines was pulled out last month. But we've learned not to get our hopes up too high. We won't believe it until it actually happens.

Joanie wrote me about her visit with you. She really enjoyed being with you all. It was also a pleasant way to spend an evening away from her studies. The senior level courses she is taking now are really difficult as far as involving a lot of time. She has so many books to read and papers to write. Most of her letters to me are written late at night or a short one sometime during the day, so I know exactly how busy she really is. That's good, though, because it makes the time go by fast. It's hard to realize that I'm already in my 7th month. The time has been going by quickly for me also. Each day seems to slip away into the dusk...

I learned that the PX in DaNang not only sells Gen. Motors, Chrysler, Ford and American Motors cars, but also that I can get a Volkswagen. I haven't been able to get into DaNang to talk about it. But from what I understand... I can buy a Volkswagen and continue paying for it after I get back to the States. That's good because we can hold the money that I've been saving as a reserve rather than using most of it to pay for the car. Joanie also wrote about a lot of garage apartments that are really nice for less than $100/month. Something like this will be good for us.

Sept. 9–16 is the date. R&R in Sydney, Australia. A friend just got back from his R&R there. He said it was really great. I really am looking forward to it.

Love,
Michael."

"11-Sept.-69

Dear Mom and Dad,
Getting short, Mom, coming home pretty soon. Going to quit flying soon, too much for me now. I went in front of a board for sp/5 will know soon if i made it. I have now 20 oak leaf clusters and some more paper for you. I have flown 1500 hours now, and in those hours I could tell you a lifetime story. I have been put in for a medal again, but this time I have seen far beyond of what ever you will see. That is why I'm going to quit flying. I dream of Valerie's hand touching mine telling me to come home; but I wake up, and it's some sergeant telling me I have to fly. Today I am 21, far away but coming home older.

Love,
Larry"

Below: A member of Company G, 2nd Battalion, 1st Marine Regiment, at An Hoa writes a letter home to his family in the United States.

In September 1969, Larry Jackson of the 129th AHC (Assault Helicopter Company) had served in Vietnam for nine months. A skilled young pilot, he had earned a number of decorations, but after 1,500 flying hours, was ready to come home. Sadly, he was killed on his 21st birthday, less than 24 hours after writing this letter.

Operation Desert Storm 1991

Even today, in the age of satellite phones and e-mail, soldiers far away from home rely on the mail. "A soldier's best friend, next to his rifle, is the postman," said Lieutenant General Walt Boomer in an interview with *Newsweek* magazine in 1990, and this is as true today as it was 200 years ago. The level of media interest in a war often awakes the sympathy and curiosity of the civilian population at home. During the Gulf War the "Any Service Mail Member" scheme was introduced, which directed letters of support or curiosity to serving soldiers, sailors, and marines. Many servicemen and women replied, providing details of their work, recording their feelings at being so far from home, and their impressions of the Middle East.

When Iraq invaded the small Gulf state of Kuwait in August 1990, the U.S. led a coalition of 30 nations in a concerted effort to restore Kuwait's independence and put an end to the aggressive posturing of Saddam Hussein, the president of Iraq. When Operation Desert Shield evolved into Operation Desert Storm in January 1991, over 500,000 U.S. troops were involved; for America, this meant 81 tons of mail per day.

"27 Oct 90

...My name is Herbert Hall I'm a Construction Mechanic third class stationed on the USS Trenton. There isn't much to tell. So far we've learned to stay out of the sun as much as possible and drink plenty of water. Other than that we are just waiting. Morale is low. The crew is bored of doing nothing. We've been underway for the past 80 days with no liberty ports. Communication with our families has much to be desired. Over all we just want something to happen. Most of the marines and sailors alike think we should go in and destroy that little country. If we don't do it now in a few years Iraq will have nuclear capabilities and we'll be right back over here, So I feel we should just get this over with so we could get home and be with our families...

Herbert Hall
U.S.S. Trenton"

Left: Two soldiers watch the sun set over the Saudi Arabian desert.

"To whom it may concern Oct 28, 1990

I am a marine serving in Operation Desert Shield 1990. Marines have been called upon in lots of crisis but never one this large. Its a very different experience in the Desert. Most of the world's conflicts have been in jungle environments. Being a marine, myself and my feelings toward the Gulf crisis is, that I think that Iraq shouldn't be allowed to take Kuwait, because its just like playing monopoly, once you get one piece of property, you get control of other properties. We are not over here to just lower gas prices for people, we are here to keep Iraq from gaining power. I have had many experiences on this operation. I've left my wife and new born son. My family and everyone I know, will worry about me until I return. We are in one of the biggest Flights of ships that's ever been together, we have 21 ships in our task force. We've passed through the Suez canal ship after ship and every ship is going over its time period to be out here, most ships were supposed to return in Oct– Nov but the Gulf Crisis will not allow it to happen. The operation is going very well, and I think it will be a success. Maybe we will be home with flying colors. Thank you and I hope to hear from you personally again.

Sincerely
L Cpl. James Holcomb
United States Marines"

"25 Jan 91

My name is SGT Craig W. Bukowski, I'm in the 890th Transportation Company out of Green Bay. I'm 22 years old and reside in Green Bay. I got off of active duty in August of 1990. I served 3 years as an Airborne Combat Engineer (12 B) at Fort Devens. I was attending College at UW Stevens Point when my reserve unit was activated on October 10.

Now I'm in Saudi Arabia driving semi trucks hauling ammunition, tank rounds, Multi Launching Rocket Systems (MLRS) and even Patriot missiles to the front line ammo dumps.

Since the war started on Jan 16, 91 we've sustained 3 SCUD missile attacks. There were no casualties thanks to the Patriot missile systems. However, it was pretty frightening to wake up at 4 A.M. to the sound of missiles exploding overhead.

My father is also over here. He's a Lieutenant Colonel with the 432nd Civil Affairs Co. His civilian job was/is the Brown County Corporation Counsel. He is a Judge Advocate General (Jag) officer and deals mainly with setting up governments and dealing with the civilians of an overthrown country.

My personal opinion is that we should be here. The liberation of Kuwait and overthrow of Iraq is essential to maintaining peace in the Gulf, as well as the rest of the world...

Craig W. Bukowski
SGT Bukowski
890th Tran. Co/68th Tran. BN
APO NY 09899"

Above: A soldier suffering heat exhaustion in the Saudi Desert is evacuated during Operation Desert Shield.

Afghanistan 2002

When Al Qaida terrorists attacked the heart of the American mainland by driving passenger aircraft into the Pentagon in Washington and the Twin Towers of the World Trade Center in New York, the nation and most of the world united behind President George W. Bush's calls for revenge. U.S. air, sea, and land troops were dispatched to Afghanistan to root out Osama bin Laden, the man behind the terrible acts of violence. When the forces of the Taliban had been defeated, a United Nations peacekeeping force, consisting of troops from 18 countries, including Britain, the U.S.A., and many E.U. states, arrived to maintain order and help Afghanistan to recover from 20 years of misrule. This letter written in February 2002, is from a female British soldier, a corporal serving in the Royal Corps of Signals who is a veteran of peacekeeping operations in Kosovo.

"The terrain is quite similar to Kosovo but not nearly as green. It is very bleak. The nights are cold as we are still living in tents but we have a heater and I sleep in three sleeping bags at the moment.

It's like another world when you drive through the so-called town. There are only a few women who show their faces and they seem so scared. They give their children and babies to the soldiers hoping they will be safer. One day I walked to the American Embassy from the camp with some American soldiers and everybody just stopped and watched my every move in shock to see a woman with a rifle and uniform. It feels so strange to be stared at like that. Luckily I don't leave the camp much as it doesn't feel safe to walk about even if we are armed... Hopefully we should be home in mid-April. I hope it's sooner as I miss home very much."

Letters from American troops show that they take Operation Enduring Freedom (the name for U.S. operations in Afghanistan) extremely seriously, often personally, and many believe they are in Afghanistan in order to make the world safe for democracy. Letters like this (first published in *Marine*

Times) express with great clarity the reasons for fighting. Marine Corps Reserve Lieutenant Colonel Tom D. Barna, comes from a family with a strong military tradition and is 45-year-old father of three. Barna spent eight months in the Persian Gulf when his son, Alex, was just two.

"Dear Son,

Right up front, let me tell you that I love you, I am proud of you, and I am safe. It's hard to believe I am over here again! When I left the desert 10 years ago, at the conclusion of the Gulf War, I just never thought I would be here again. When I was here last time, I was an active-duty captain in the Marine Corps. This time I return as a lieutenant colonel in the Marine Corps Reserve.

I've joked with your mom about not being sure which was worse —leaving her alone with three babies [during the Gulf War] or leaving her behind with three teenagers. I can still hear her laughing.

Son, my deployment seems a little more personal this time. As you know, it was our nation that was attacked. It was our people who died. And this fire has been brewing for quite a while. I think all Americans are finally ready to rid the world of men bent on imposing their evil will. This time it's different... this time we just won't take it! This time we finish the fight.

I will be honest with you: Nothing in my life is greater than

Right: U.S. special forces troops ride horseback as they work with members of the Northern Alliance in Afghanistan during Operation Enduring Freedom in November 2001.

serving the Corps, God and country. But I am here for another reason, too—a reason that personally motivates me. I am here so you won't one day have to come back and finish something we didn't take care of here and now.

Your grandpa served in Korea and in Southeast Asia and is buried at Arlington National Cemetery. He fought so that I could live in a world of peace... and men and women like him ended the Cold War. Now it's my turn, along with men and women of my time. We must be at war, to once and for all bring a time where our children—that's you, Alex—can live in a world of real peace.

This one is for you!

I so very much miss you, your sisters and your mom. I'll be home soon. We'll all be home soon. In the meantime, I will pray for you and dream of you often.

Love,
Dad"

Letters and parcels continue to sustain the morale of troops thousands of miles from home. Airman 1st Class Marco D. Nario of the 621st Tanker Airlift Control Element writes via the (*Airforce Times*) from the U.S. military outpost at Bagram air base, Afghanistan.

"Hello Mom, Dad, Brothers, Sisters, Family and Friends,

Just want to let you know how grateful and pleased I am to be part of your life. Reading your letters and opening the packages you send truly lifts me when I'm down and warms me when I feel lonely. In return, here I am on the other side of the world dedicating my time and service to eliminate the terrorism that disfigured our way of life. I'm fighting not only for America, but also for the whole world that desires to have peace in their hearts and minds.

I never thought that at a very young age I would be participating in a war that would bring forth joy, peace and a lovely world for tomorrow's children. I truly believe that we can win this battle not only because we have the best technology, but also because we have integrity in all things. Not only do we have the best weapons, but we

learn how to sacrifice ourselves for others. And not only are we well-trained, but we also aim to be excellent in everything.

I may not know what lies ahead tomorrow. It may be pleasant or painful. But this I know, my life is in God's hands. If God is with us, therefore, who can be against us?

Thank you for keeping us in prayer and remember that I love you all, I miss you all, and I can't wait to be with you all again!

God bless,
Marco"

Soldiers across the world and throughout history share a similar professional ethos and take pride in their work. They also express the same hopes and fears in time of war: that they will win, that their relatives will not worry, and that they will survive to be sent home quickly. This letter from Lance Corporal Joshua Phillips (via the *Marine Times*) sums up all this in a few short paragraphs. Serving with the 3rd Battalion, 6th Marines, 26th Marine Expeditionary, Phillips was based in Kandahar, Afghanistan, during Operation Enduring Freedom.

"Hey there!

How are y'all doing? I'm fine and in good health. Right now I'm sitting outside my fighting position at Kandahar International Airport. We moved into Afghanistan about six days ago now. We are setting a defensive perimeter around the airfield so that we can get support in and land C-130s and C-5s.

The weather is warm during the day and very cold at night, but we'll manage. I'm not sure when we're getting out of here. I've heard as early as Dec. 28 and as late as Jan. 20. But the happy medium that they seem to be sticking with is Jan. 10. Tell Brittney I love and miss her. I can't wait to get back on ship and give y'all a call! I love y'all so much and miss you just as much. Take care of yourselves and the critters and don't worry too much! I love y'all! Take care!

Love,
Josh"

Credits

Select Bibliography

Anderson, Duncan. *Military Elites*. London: Bison Books, 1995

Boyden, Peter. *Tommy Atkins' Letters*. London: National Army Museum, 1990

Connor, Ken. *Ghost Force*. London: Weidenfeld & Nicolson, 1998

Encyclopedia of American History. New York: Harpur & Rowe, 1982

Evans, Martin Matrix. *Passchendaele & the Battles of Ypres 1914–18*. London: Osprey, 1997

Everett, Susanne. *World War I*. London: Bison Books, 1980

Foote, Shelby. *The Civil War, A Narrative*. London: Pimlico, 1992

Frémont-Barnes, Gregory. *The French Revolutionary Wars*. London: Osprey, 2001

Glover, Michael. *Battlefields of Northern France and the Low Countries*. London: Michael Joseph Ltd, 1987

Hibbert, Christopher. *Wellington A Personal History*. London: HarperCollins, 1998

Katcher, Philip. *The American Civil War Source Book*. London: Arms and Armour Press, 1992

Keegan, John. *The Face of Battle*. London: Pimlico, 1976

Keegan, John, *The First World War*. London: Hutchinson, 1998

Lee, Robert E. *Letters of General Lee by Captain Robert E. Lee, His Son*. London: Book Sales, 1988.

Longford, Elizabeth. *Wellington Years of the Sword*. London: Weidenfeld & Nicolson, 1969

MacDonald, Lyn. *1914–1918 Voice & Images of the Great War*. London: Penguin, 1991

Morison, Commager and Leuchtenburg. *The Growth of the American Republic*. Oxford: OUP, 1980

Morrissey, Brendan. *Boston 1775*. London: Osprey, 1993

Companion to Military History. London: Osprey, 1999

Pimlott, John. *Atlas of Warfare*. London: Bison Books, 1988

Regan, Geoffrey. *The Guinness Book of Military Blunders*. London: Guinness Publishing, 1991

Sherman, William T. *Memoirs of General William T. Sherman*. London: Penguin, 2000.

Young, Peter (Ed.). *The World Almanac of World War II*. London, Bison Books, 1981

Web sites

www.swcivilwar.com

www.tngenweb.org/tnletters/tx/mex002.htm

www.iaw.on.ca/~jsek/1812maas.htm

www.galafilm.com

www.military.com

www.hillsdale.edu/dept/History/Documents

We have made every effort possible to trace the copyright holders of the letters reproduced in this book.
   Thanks are due to the following institutions for permission to reproduce historic documents from their web sites:

Army Times Publishing Company (*www.militarycity.com*),
   Airman 1st Class Marco D. Nario, Marine Corps Reserve Lt. Col. Tom D. Barna, L/Cpl. Joshua Phillips, 2001

The Clements Library, University of Michigan (*www.si.umich.edu/spies/*):
   Rachel Revere to Paul Revere, 1775, George Washington about denture repairs, 1781

Hillsdale College History Dept website and David Stewart (*www.hillsdale.edu/dept/History/Documents*):
   Lt. Col. Smith's report of Lexington, 1775, Lt Waller, battle of Bunker Hill, Maj. Gen. Burgoyne to his nieces, 1777, Lt. Hale on an officer's life, 1778, Maj. Warre, 1809, Lt. Col. Ponsonby, Salamanca, 1809, Isaac Chauncey naval battle of York, Fort Dearborn Massacre, Battle of River Raisin, 1813, Tingey Attack on Washington, 1814, George B. McClellan, 1846

Imperial War Museum (Trustees)
   Rosmund DuCrane: Papers of Lt. John Staniforth

Kansas State Historical Society (*www.kshs.org*)
   Roy Bainbridge, 1918, John A. Martin, 1944, Ensign Paul Stephens, 1945, Dr Robert Feighny, 1964

Leicestershire Country Archives
   The Freer Letters, 1809

Library of Congress
   Giles S Thomas, 1863, John Kennedy to Claire Booth Luce, 1942, Stalin on Second Front, 1942

Military Advantage, Inc, (*www.military.com*)
   General Lewis Puller, 1950

Nottinghamshire County Archive
   Letter of Charles Stanley, 1815

ublic Record Office

    Wellington's Waterloo Dispatch, Churchill 1944 memo, 1941 memo re intelligence security, Wavell's last order from Singapore, Percival's order from Singapore

irginia Military Institute Archives Lexington, Virginia (*www.vmi.edu*)

    Stonewall Jackson, Vera Cruz, 1847, Stonewall Jackson, Mexico, 1848, P G T Beauregard Fort Sumter, 1861, Henry Campbell 1st Bull Run , Stonewall Jackson, 1862 , Pvt. Dedrick on Jackson and conditions in the army, 1863, Lt. Col. Willliam Bentley Southern provisions, Napoleon B. Brisbane, 1864 Prisoner of War

he War Times Journal and Jim Burbeck (*www.wtj.com*)

    Nelson's despatch from the battle of Nile 1798 and his letters to Lady Hamilton and Horatia, Napoleon's Waterloo orders, Wellington's condolences to Lord Aberdeen

isconsin Veterans Museum Archives and Research Center

    Desert Storm veterans' letters

Acknowledgments

would like to express my gratitude for the kindness and generosity shown by many people who have

    aned their family letters and been kind enough to allow me to use them in this book. In

    etical order:

    for the Freer correspondence.

    n for the First World War letters of his father Capt. Leslie Green;

    ominski for his letter from Vietnam;

    Jackson for the Vietnam letter of his brother pilot Larry Jackson;

    Lofgren, Editor, Corson-Sioux News/Messenger;

    nk Mack for the letters of Cpl Francis Mack;

    /Cpl Angela Nicholls;

    ul O'Connell for his letters from Vietnam;

    an McAninch Samuelson for the Vietnam letters of Michael McAninch;

    ff Staley for the letters of Lloyd Staley;

    ichard Stillwell for the 1915 letter of L/Cpl Cecil East, the 1940-42 letters of Lt. John Stillwell and Major Bill Stillwell;

    ene Towner for the 1812 letters of Ensign Thomas Warner.

Picture Credits

he publisher wishes to thank the following for kindly supplying the images for this book:

hoto by Lt. Wayne Miller, supplied courtesy of the National Archives (Control Number NWDNS-80-G-469517; Still Pictures Branch (NWDNS), National Archives at College Park, 8601 Adelphi Road, College Park, MD): 2, 3, 111;

Hulton|Archive: 4-5, 9, 13(inset), 15, 22, 23, 24 (background), 25, 26, 27, 29 (top and bottom), 30, 31 (top and bottom), 32, 36, 37, 38, 41, 46-47(background), 47(inset), 48, 49, 54, 58 (top and bottom), 60-61 (background), 61(inset), 62, 64 (top and bottom), 66, 67, 90-91 (background), 106, 117, 130;

©Tim Page/ Corbis : 6-7 ;

©Bettmann/ Corbis: 8, 62, 73, 97 (top and bottom), 100, 122 ;

Photo from the Historical Section of the War Plans Division, War Department. Supplied courtesy of the National Archives (Control Number NWDNS-165-WW-556B(23); Still Pictures Branch (NWDNS), National Archives at College Park, 8601 Adelphi Road, College Park, MD): 10;

Images are reproduced by courtesy of the Public Record Office [Crown Copyright material in the Public Record Office] is reproduced by permission of the controller of Her Majesty's Stationary Office : 12 (inset),12-13 (background),19, 24 (inset),40, 42, 46 (inset), 60 (inset),90(inset), 108-109 (background and inset), 112, 113;

©Archio Iconografico, S.A/Corbis: 28 (left);

©Francis G Mayer/Corbis: 28 (right);

Gene Towner: 50, 51, 52, 53;

Chrysalis Images: 68 (inset), 85, 86, 124, 126 (inset), 126-127(background), 127 (inset), 129, 138, 139 ;

©Corbis : 68-69 (background), 70, 75, 81, 82, 83, 89, 98 (top), 121 (top and bottom) ;

©Medford Historical Society Collection/ Corbis: 69 (inset), 71, 78;

Nebraska State Historical Society (Digital ID nbhips l006): 80;

©Hulton-Deutsch collection/ Corbis: 91(inset), 92, 94, 98 (bottom), 103;

Kansas State Historical Society: 102, 116(left and right), 118, 119, 131;

Harry S Truman Library : 104,105, 107 ;

Stillwell Collection : 110, 114 ;

Manuscript Division, Library of Congress (Reproduction number: A60 (color slide; pages 1-4): 115;

W. Averell Harriman Papers, Manuscript Divison, Library of Congress (Reproduction number: A47 (color slide; pages 1 and 2)): 120;

Denver Public Library, Western History Collection. Photo by Richard A. Rocker: 123 (right);

Karl Winkelmann 123(left), 125;

Military Archive and Research Services: 132, 133, 134, 136;

Photo by John A. Gentry, LCpl, supplied courtesy of the National Archives (Control Number NWDNS-127-N-A372113; Still Pictures Branch (NWDNS), National Archives at College Park, 8601 Adelphi Road, College Park, MD): 137;

Department of Defense : 140 ;

For front and back cover acknowledgments please see jacket.

Index